McKenzie

To Alfredo,

Impossible is <u>nothing</u>!
Always believe in yourself
and chase your dreams!

your friend,

Mckenzie

Breaking Free

Shattering Expectations and Thriving With Ambition in Pursuit of Gold

Author: McKenzie Coan

Contributing Author: Holly Neumann

Editor: Marla McKenna

Associate Editor: Lyda Rose Haerle

Cover Design: Nicole Wurtele
Graphic Designer with The CG Sports Company

Interior Layout: Michael Nicloy

All Photos courtesy of McKenzie Coan unless otherwise noted

Cover Photos: Brandon Johnson Photography

Published by CG Sports Publishing

Head of Publishing: Michael Nicloy

Marketing Coordinator: Rachel Draffen

Director of Marketing for The CG Sports Company

A Division of The CG Sports Company

Cejih Yung, CEO and Founder

www.cgsportsco.com

ISBN: 978-1-7359193-2-4

Quantity order requests can be emailed to Matt Amerlan:
Publishing@cgsportsmanagement.com

Printed in The United States of America

"*This book will make you question what you complain about. McKenzie Coan has been an example of positive attitude in the face of constant adversity. From a young child, to the pinnacle of sport, the challenges that she's faced have been met head on and overcome by herself and her entire family. This book will give you a greater perspective on the journey of this amazing Paralympic Champion.*"

- Glenn Mills (1980 US Olympic Swimmer, Owner of GoSwim.com)

"*McKenzie's ability to persevere through what most would consider career-ending circumstances not only speaks to McKenzie's strength as a person but also her undeniable grit and determination that she developed from a very young age. But what's extra special about her is how she has a way of making everyone around her feel as if they can achieve anything, too. Through* Breaking Free, *the world gets to experience McKenzie's truly magical spirit and presence.*"

- Kara Lynn Joyce, three-time U.S. Olympian

For Mom, Dad, Grant, and Eli. Thank you for always believing in me. Your love and support have carried me through my darkest days and lifted me up in my happiest moments.

FOREWORD

The 2012 London Paralympic Games were the first I attended as a member of the United States Paralympic swimming coaching staff. Those Games opened the eyes of the world to the Paralympics with unprecedented media coverage and amazing athletic performances. The motto of the Games was "Inspire a Generation," and it was at these London Games that I first met McKenzie Coan. It was also there that I saw the beginning of McKenzie's barrier-breaking journey from high school student to college student to Paralympic gold medalist and world record holder.

Prior to 2007, I had no knowledge of what the Paralympic Games were, nor did I have much interaction with disabled swimmers. I had been an able-bodied coach of able-bodied swimmers for my 12-year coaching career at Loyola University Maryland. That all changed one day when Philip Scholz, a blind swimmer from Mt. Sinai, New York, walked into my office and asked if he could join the college team as a walk-on. Since that day, I have had the privilege to coach 10 Paralympians, at least one in each of the Paralympic Games since 2008. These athletes have combined to reach the Paralympic podium 18 times with eight gold medals. After the 2016 Rio Paralympic Games, McKenzie Coan would be the most decorated woman I have coached to date.

Big Mac, MC Hammer, Kenzie, Mac, Small Fry, KC, Mac n Cheese, and Golden Mermaid. These are all nicknames I have heard McKenzie Coan called over the years. Each one reveals a small portion of her personality to the world. Golden Mermaid was coined by the Japanese news media after they saw her beautiful swimming stroke.

For me though, she has always been McKenzie with the infectious and eternal smile that she wears in and out of the pool. I have been blessed to see this smile the past several years at swim practice, meets, and my daily interactions with her. No matter if she is finishing a hard swimming set, speaking with elementary school children, or lending a helping hand to a teammate, she optimizes kindness and positivity. She bears her beautiful smile despite the daily challenges she faces as part of what is her "normal" life.

Breaking Free—Shattering Expectations and Thriving With Ambition in Pursuit of Gold will be seen as an inspirational story much like the 2012 Paralympic London Games motto, "Inspire a Generation." The realities are that this story is so much more. Through this book, McKenzie aspires to change how disabled individuals are perceived. To say McKenzie is an inspiration, though, would be selling her short. McKenzie is a Paralympic gold medalist, world record holder, sponsored professional athlete, college graduate, NCAA Division I swimmer, law school candidate, author, and amazing individual. She is all of these and a woman with a disability. Her disability does not define who she is but is just part of her life.

Reading this book will help you see how an amazing family and community never doubted what McKenzie could achieve. From early on, McKenzie's parents allowed her to pursue her passions and didn't let her disability hinder her pursuit of excellence.

Years from now, when McKenzie is retired as a swimmer and I as a coach, we will still be able to refer to this book to touch a new generation of individuals.

Buckle up and get ready for the journey in McKenzie's words!

Brian Loeffler
Head Swimming and Diving Coach, Loyola University Maryland
2014 Paralympic Coach of the Year

There's literally nothing stopping you—
the only limitations that exist are
the ones that you allow to exist.

McKenzie

No one prepares you for the little things: where to stand, exactly, when the flag is raised, for instance, or what to do with your hands. After years of imagining this moment, I found myself forgetting the obvious—step back with the others, hold the stuffed toy they hand you—and worrying about my shoes.

One was loose, but it's not like I was going to bend over in front of everybody and tie it.

No one tells you, either, how heavy a gold medal is or how when you lean to have it placed around your neck, it's weighty enough to knock you off-balance.

That would have been good information.

A slight wobble later, though, I stood solidly at the front of the podium and took in the moment. The American flag rose, and the *Star-Spangled Banner* played. I sang through my giant smile and streaming tears.

I had done it. And, it turns out, I'd do it twice more at that Paralympic Games in Rio de Janeiro in 2016, achieving the rare feat of winning every freestyle event offered in my classification, the 50-, 100- and 400-meter races. It's called winning the Triple, and as unlikely as it is, my accomplishment was just the latest in a lifetime of unlikeliness.

That first medal came after the women's S7 50-meter freestyle, a sprint to the far wall and not my usual forte. The second was for my favorite event, my baby, the 400-meter freestyle. The third, in the 100, left me feeling awash in pride, relief, and gratitude. I hadn't gotten there alone. As "the land of the free and the home of the brave" rang over loudspeakers, memories flooded my brain.

One stood out: the day my mother dramatically chucked my life jacket toward a poolside garbage bin, and freedom and bravery got personal.

CHAPTER ONE

BIRTH TO 5

"Swim," my mother said as she lowered me into the water of the competition pool in our rural Georgia town. I did because it was what I desperately wanted—a chance to try out for the Habersham Rapids Swim Team, my brothers' club. I wanted to be like my siblings, which is a perfectly normal wish for a 5-year-old, but this tryout was far from the norm.

Both Coach Anthony Rayburn and my mother were scared to death.

It wasn't just because I was so young or even that I had never before swum without a life jacket. It was my disability, osteogenesis imperfecta, that had everyone holding their breath.

Osteogenesis imperfecta, or OI, is a genetic disorder that results in brittle bones. It means the slightest of bumps or twists can result in a fracture, and in my short life I'd had plenty of them. Playing in the water helped strengthen my body, so while my brothers, Grant and Eli, attended swim team practice, I attended water therapy in the adjacent warm-water pool, always in a life vest, always with my mom nearby.

But I had my sights set on bigger things: a dream put in motion that summer at an Applebee's and confirmed with a pinkie promise.

"So, when are you going to join the Rapids?" Coach Rayburn had asked me at a team dinner after the Georgia state meet, where we had watched my brother Grant swim.

It was the kind of friendly, coach-kid interaction that I suspect most adults would not remember. Coach Anthony says he doesn't. But he had made me feel welcome and wanted, so the idea of swim team stuck. I told him, "Soon," and we sealed the deal by hooking our little fingers above a plate of fries.

My mother gave in after I argued that my brother Eli was younger than me, and he was on the team. How unfair was it that I was relegated to playtime in the "baby pool"?

"No more life jacket, no matter what," my mother said on the day of the tryout, tossing the vest in the direction of the can. "We're all in or we're all out."

I was all in. Just to put any doubts to rest, I swam six lengths of the pool without stopping, even though only a single 25-yard swim was required to earn a spot on the team.

Still, I balked a little before the first practice. (I was only 5, after all.)

"I'm not sure I want to do this," I told my mom.

"Too bad," she said. "You just signed up for something, and you'll now finish the season."

Clearly, she was all in, too.

How hard was it for my mother to let me join the swim team? To answer that question, it's best to start at the beginning, June 1996, when I was born with a broken leg.

They didn't really know it was broken at first, but everyone could tell something was different about me.

My father, Marc Coan, is an internist, and his best friend, Mike Maley, who would become my Godfather, is a pediatrician. So when I was born, they both could see right away that something was up. But what? I was full term but super small, and the bones in my skull were what's called Wormian. My mom says they were soft and "basically not there." I was also very bow-legged.

The doctors at the hospital, Mike, and my dad all suspected hypothyroidism. But I tested negative for that, and they sent us home.

Nineteen days later, after a 4 a.m. feeding, my mother was burping me, and she heard a "pop."

She laid me on the bed and looked.

Oh, dear God. I think she has a broken leg, my mom remembers thinking. She consoled me and woke up my dad. He looked at me, and then her.

"Teresa, tell me you dropped her," he said.

"I did not drop this child," she replied.

Off to the ER they went, and so began what my mother calls her "merry-go-round."

Mike and an orthopedic doctor arrived at the hospital, and it was determined I had a broken leg. ("Duh," my mom says now.) Then, referring to a reference book as they talked, they told my parents about osteogenesis imperfecta.

"OK. Fine," my mom remembers saying. "Load her up with some calcium, and let's get going."

She was told there was no cure.

We were sent home with a teeny-tiny fiberglass cast on my lower leg. Not long after, while sitting in my mother's lap, I squirmed and stretched a bit, and the weight of the honeycomb-looking cast broke my femur (the bone in the upper part of the leg).

Dear God, give me strength, my mother prayed.

The strength wasn't for herself. It was for me.

Lots of tests followed. At some point, it was found that I'd broken my femur for the first time in utero, the umbilical cord having snaked around my leg and snapped it. (That explained why my mother felt my kicking stop when she was pregnant, even though she'd been assured that my vitals were strong.)

A geneticist performed a skin biopsy, which confirmed my OI diagnosis and showed that I have a severe form of the condition. Typically, people with my type of OI have brittle bones and often scoliosis, which is a curvature of the spine. They may have dwarfism (short stature); have a barrel-shaped chest, leading to respiratory vulnerabilities; and may develop hearing loss due to bone deformity and deterioration in the inner ear. I have all these traits. (I have asthma, too, which is unrelated to OI, but it compounds my lung troubles.)

My parents were told I would never sit, stand, walk, or even talk, if I lived past infancy. It was a devastating outlook.

Osteogenesis imperfecta is usually inherited, but it can't be traced in either of my parents' bloodlines. The geneticist told them that my having OI was the outcome of a spontaneous mutation.

That doctor was also the first person to tell them, "What a beautiful little girl you have."

The skin biopsy left a scar on my left arm. I call it my "mutant mark" as a reminder that OI happened for me—not to me. The distinction is important because while OI is scary and difficult, OI is what makes me, me.

After my diagnosis, my mother suffered through a period of guilt (even though my OI was no one's fault) and a steep learning curve. She used cushions to pack me into places, so I wouldn't accidentally bump into the side of, say, a baby seat. When she held me, I lay on top of a pillow, so I was surrounded in softness. She sewed my clothing because regular baby clothes were too tricky to pull on and off. I couldn't wear shoes—the weight of them could break me—so she dressed me in frilly socks because she wanted me to have special things.

Mom learned to not panic when I broke something. She carried Ace bandages and popsicle sticks in her purse—and later tongue depressors as I grew—to splint breaks on the fly. My brother Grant, just 2½ years older than me, was often her assistant, and he quickly became more skilled than nurses at stabilizing a broken bone. (Is it any wonder he's in medical school now?)

Every task concerning me—diapering, feeding, burping, bathing—had to be done gingerly, deliberately, and often completely differently than how my mom had taken care of my brother as infant. She had to figure out how to adapt on her own. There was no one to help her who knew anything more than she did.

Even with such care, at six months, the list of my missed milestones was long. I could not hold up my head, for instance, so we were referred to a physical therapist, Colleen Coulter, who had experience with OI children.

When we arrived, Colleen took me from my mother's arms, a bold move, considering my mother's protectiveness. Even my dad hardly ever held me.

My mother was stunned.

"You can put her on a shelf like a China doll," Colleen told my mother, "or you can let her live."

My mom considers this a turning point, and she says it was the first truly hopeful moment since I'd been born. It helped her to realize how she was going to parent me and my brothers. We were all equal parts of the family. The family would not revolve around my needs or me. And she would be all in, for all of us.

With Colleen's help, my mother learned exercises to encourage me to hold up my head and eventually sit. Mom made decorative, fancy eye patches when I needed to wear one because I had a weak eye. Grant was included in our daily routines, and he wore a shiny eye patch, too, because he thought that these were the types of things every brother did.

There were gains, and there were setbacks.

One day after I was a year old, I lay on my parents' bed, surrounded by pillows while my mom got ready for the day. The barriers were up mostly just to keep Grant out. I was immobile, after all, right?

Wrong. That was the day I decided to learn to crawl.

A crash to the floor landed me in my first hip spica body cast, a milestone no one wants to experience. There was concern about skull fractures, too. The fall also deeply shook my mother.

She was put in touch with a woman in Tennessee, another mother of an OI child.

"I don't know how to do this," she confessed over the phone to her support mom, Juanita.

"Honey," Juanita said, "you're going to do fine."

Those early years were full of fits and starts, like they are for any family with young children, but I expect ours were a bit…extra. My brother Eli was born when I was 18 months old, so there were soon three of us for my mom to wrangle.

Eli and I are very close—we could be twins, if it weren't for, well, the obvious age difference and his not having OI. When my mom was pregnant with him, she endured judgy questions about why and how she was having another child. Of course, that's no one's business, but true story: Eli did give her a significant scare once when he kicked from the womb, and my mom heard a telltale "pop!"

I'm going to have another child with OI! she worried.

Turns out, Eli had kicked so forcefully, he had broken my mother's rib!

Maybe that was a sign. My mom says I was "not always angelic," and Eli quickly became my "henchman." If I needed something from up high—a cookie or toy, for example—Eli would climb to get it, especially if I agreed to share it with him. He's also at least 50 percent responsible for a broken arm I once got while playing football in the house.

My brothers were my first cheerleaders. Grant, always dependable and serious, led the way, and Eli, ever the wildcard, provided enough entertainment to keep things fun. Grant and Eli never knew what it might be like to not have a sibling with a disability, and I've never heard them complain about accommodating my needs, even when it meant spending days at my hospital bedside. My parents adopted some advice from Juanita: whenever I was laid up with an injury or illness, I would have 24-48 hours, once I came home, to return to being a productive part of the family. I'm sure this helped keep the peace, and the Coan kids made a great team.

My first surgery was when I was 2½ years old. I had learned to walk using a walker, and once, when I tried to run, I fell. I had a spiral fracture in my leg that time, which basically means my bone was shredded. A rodding surgery would be required to repair it.

The idea was that the surgeon would place a metal rod inside my leg, which would become like an internal splint. The fear was that my bone would disintegrate upon this attempt. They planned for my needing a blood transfusion, and they warned my mother the surgery would take a while.

It did. And then, it took longer.

"What is going on?" my mother paced from where she waited. She prayed for news.

When the call finally came, the news was good. My bone hadn't fallen apart. No transfusion had been needed.

"What took so long, then?" she wanted to know.

That's when she learned I'd demanded a very specific color for my body cast, and they had to specially create it. Maybe that was a sign, too. From an early age, I knew what I wanted.

CHAPTER TWO

THAT SWIM LIFE

The Habersham Rapids team practices at the Ruby C. Fulbright Aquatic Center in my hometown of Clarkesville, Georgia, a city of fewer than 2,000 people in the hilly northeast corner of the state. That such a modern aquatics facility existed in such a small city, and that it housed a USA Swimming program, was serendipitous. From when it opened in 2001, the Coans were fixtures at Ruby Fulbright.

I loved swim team. Coach Anthony treated me like any other kid, an intuitive strategy for my success that he credits to his own naivety. He worried about my maybe hitting my heels on the pool's gutters when I flip-turned, but he didn't put me in a special lane or keep me from fully participating. Kids learned to be careful, and it's amazing no one ever collided with me in a circle-swimming snafu.

(Circle swimming is the way multiple swimmers can share a lane. Done correctly, it's like driving—stay to the right side of the middle line. But it's common for swimmers to absent-mindedly stray to the wrong side of the lane and run into each other. That would be a disaster for me. Luckily, I had good lane mates.)

Coach Anthony says he didn't do much to adapt my workouts, either, other than to do what made sense. My arms were strong from pushing my wheelchair, which I used more than walking on my own. My legs were weaker, often in ski-boot-like braces, which made me clumsy, so the wheelchair was safer a lot of the time. This is still the case today, minus the braces.

Some of my best memories of those early swim years are of swim meets with my friends, dressed up in our bright-orange team gear, talking about "Hannah Montana," and playing games on the pool deck. Swimming was fun, and it wasn't long before I was climbing up in the results. That made it even better! When I started passing able-bodied swimmers, it fueled my desire for more.

One of my favorite swims of my career, ranked right up there with my world records, was at a meet when I was 8 years old.

I won the 100-yard individual medley (one length of the pool for each stroke—butterfly, backstroke, breaststroke, and freestyle). After the race, I tried to shake the hand of the girl in the next lane.

"The girl in the wheelchair beat me!" she bawled.

Yeah, that's right, I thought. *A little, pink wheelchair, too.*

My competitiveness came into play outside the pool, too.

No one was going to sell more Girl Scout cookies than me, or beat me at air hockey, for instance, and I worked hard academically to keep up with Grant, which was nearly impossible because he kept sneaking our homeschooling books and reading ahead. I was extremely driven in everything I did, which helped me to develop the grit and determination I needed when things were tough.

Tough, like when I was on pamidronate.

I started receiving pamidronate therapy when I was preschool-aged. Pamidronate is a medicine that was administered as an infusion into my arm over a period of three days in the hospital, and it basically added layers to my bones. In fact, when you look at my X-rays now, you can see rings on my skeleton that can be counted like tree rings, each signifying a pamidronate treatment.

I did this every few months for a decade or more, which meant that every 12 weeks, I had to pack up and plan to be away from home, swimming, and my friends, knowing that the drug made me nauseous and weak for many days to weeks after. My mother never lied to me about how difficult it was going to be, but she helped me to see the upside.

"You're going to the hospital, yes," she would say, "but you're not sick."

She was right. I could take pamidronate because I was healthy enough to handle the treatment.

So we made each hospital stay like a party. We decorated my room with balloons and butterflies, colorful blankets, and holiday decorations. We played music and movies, and we brought homemade presents and coloring books and crayons to the other kids, many of whom were gravely ill.

Eli and Grant would watch TV with me, and my dad would let me paint his fingernails. My dad worked at the hospital and people knew him, so the nurses would poke fun: "Ooooh. Lookin' good, Dr. Coan!"

Once my treatment started, though, I often was seriously sick myself, throwing up, and running a fever. My bones would ache deep inside. I needed help to hold up my head or go to the bathroom. All I would want to do is get back to the pool, where the water would free me and make me feel strong again.

Swimming quickly became what our family did. Grant was developing into a middle-distance freestyler and Eli a sprinter. We practiced every day, and weekends often meant hours-long swim meets many miles from home.

I had to be careful in unfamiliar facilities, as they were not always the most accessible or safe for me. I developed a system I called "the slick test," which I still use today. At every new pool, I wet my foot at the pool's edge and then rubbed it on the deck a little bit.

Oh, this is a slick one, I might think, and I'd be sure to use my wheelchair most of the time, to lower the risk that I might slip. Slipping would be a nightmare.

I was also often unfamiliar to other teams and swimmers, and while people were mostly kind, my mom remembers some who were not, and that still stings.

So while I got along well enough in able-bodied swimming, when I was 8 years old, three years after I ditched my life jacket, I found where I truly could shine.

I had just swum my first 500-yard freestyle race (20 lengths of the pool), which is a fairly big-kid event for an 8-year-old. I was already showing my affinity for longer races, where my mental toughness and overall fitness could eclipse others' speed and strength.

We were poolside when my mother and I saw a woman and a man in white shirts and blue pants—meet officials—coming toward us.

Uh-oh, we thought. *Were we not supposed to be where we were? What trouble were we in?*

Turns out, Coach Anthony had sent them our direction.

"Do you swim?" the woman asked me, as she introduced herself as Glenda Orth to my mother and me. Her name tag said "Goddess," though, and there was never a truer nickname. Little did I know then that this "Goddess" was about to become one of my angels.

We listened as Glenda and Pete Junkins, the other official, told us about Blaze Sports.

We learned that Blaze provides recreation and competition through adaptive sports for people who have physical disabilities—mostly kids, but also adults, many whom are disabled veterans. Today, it has international reach, but it was founded in Georgia as a legacy program of the 1996 Paralympics in Atlanta.

The Paralympic Games is the pinnacle of competition for disabled athletes. The first Paralympics was in Rome in 1960, and since 1998, it has taken place in the same cities and venues as the

Olympics. "Para" is taken from Greek, meaning "parallel," in this case to the Olympics. Swimming has been part of the Paralympics since the beginning, and it's one of now 28 sports sanctioned by the International Paralympic Committee.

Glenda and Pete had been officials for the Atlanta Games and were always looking for new Blaze swimmers. They thought I would be a good fit for the Blaze program.

"But what about the Rapids?" I asked.

I wouldn't have to leave the Rapids, Glenda and Pete assured us. Blaze practiced only once a week, so my other workouts would be with the Rapids. I could still go to meets with the Rapids, but Blaze offered me a chance to compete even more often by swimming in para swim meets, too, against people who were disabled similarly to me.

It sounded like I could get the best of both swimming worlds.

When we got home, my mom and I spent some time researching Blaze and para swimming. When I looked at the internet and saw pictures of disabled athletes with gold medals on podiums, I was inspired in a way I'd never been before. "Yes. Definitely," I told my mom, "I want to try out for Blaze."

I remember being nervous when I first joined.

Blaze coach Fred Lambeck was nervous, too, and not just for obvious reasons.

"I had a little bit of paranoia in the beginning," he says now, in his sweet, Southern twang. "I knew a little bit about OI, so I knew it was serious. But there was also that whistle!"

My mother has many talents, among them an unbelievably shrill whistle. She uses only her teeth, tongue, and lips, and it is loud.

She doesn't whistle willy-nilly, though. She has a different and distinct call for each of us Coan kids. When she whistles, we know exactly whose attention she is trying to get, and, boy, do we snap to it.

For me, she might whistle when she notices a danger ahead. Like, I could be a pool-length away, and she'll realize I'm headed for some sort of trouble—maybe a kid not paying attention or running. She'll whistle my whistle to let me know to "watch out!"

She also whistles to cheer for us from the stands at swim meets, to let us know she's in the building. My aunt once recognized her whistling the "Charge!" song among the crowd noise during a Paralympic Games broadcast on TV.

So Coach Fred, who graciously helped initiate us into para swimming, had a somewhat startling initiation of his own, too.

We had so many questions for Coach Fred, Glenda, and Pete. How are para swimming and able-bodied swimming the same? How are they different? Who would I be swimming against? Where and when are the para meets?

With their help, and with a lot of research, we got answers to some of our immediate questions:

- Para swimming and able-bodied swimming both have events for the four competitive strokes, but there might be different rules for those strokes. For instance, regular butterfly requires two arms to enter and exit the water in sync. A para swimmer doing butterfly might have an exception to this rule, depending on the swimmer's disability, like, if one arm is weaker than the other, or if the swimmer has only one arm to begin with.

- In able-bodied swimming, kids compete against others of similar age in established age groups. Boys swim against boys, and girls swim against girls. In para swimming, competition is between gendered groups that share common levels of disability. These levels are called "classifications," and there are 14 of them.

■ In para swimming, records are kept by class and gender, meaning there can be up to 14 world records for a single distance and stroke, per gender.

■ Para swimming sets its own rules and sanctions its own meets under its own national governing body, U.S. Paralympic Swimming, thus operating separately from USA Swimming, which governs age-group able-bodied swimming and the U.S. national team. U.S. Paralympic Swimming sponsors its own national team made up of Paralympic Games veterans and hopefuls.

■ Para meets take place all over the country and world, but they are not offered as frequently as able-bodied meets. For me, this meant I'd look forward to a few trips a year to places like Houston and Minneapolis to compete in para meets. Airplanes, hotels, and restaurants plus swimming? Sign me up!

The classification system is probably the most complicated part of para swimming. The 14 classifications differentiate both type of disability and how much the disability impacts the swimmer. The classes are labeled with the letter "S" for "sport" and a number.

Physical impairments are classified S1-S10. Visual impairments are given S11-S13. Intellectual impairments are classed S14.

In general, the higher the number, the less disabled a swimmer is. So an S10 is less affected by their disability when they swim than an S1. An S13 swimmer can see better than an S11. Swimmers who receive an S14 classification generally have disabilities that affect their reaction time, or they have difficulties with pattern recognition or sequencing.

It is possible, too, to have more than one classification. If someone's disability affects them more for say, breaststroke (likely, in this case, because of limited range of motion in the hips—breaststroke has a frog-like kick), that swimmer would compete in a more disabled class for breaststroke than they do for other strokes.

The people who evaluate swimmers for their level of disability are called classifiers. They usually are volunteers who have a background in physical therapy or exercise science. They might be doctors, parents of para swimmers, or former para swimmers themselves. Whatever their background, they go through extensive training to learn how to determine a swimmer's class.

I can only imagine how hard it must be to not only master body mechanics but also specific disabilities. I have the utmost respect for classifiers. There's a level of trust, integrity, and honesty that exists between the classifiers and athletes so that the system works and honors the spirit of the Paralympic movement.

Still, my experience with the classification process has been sometimes frustrating and oftentimes scary because so few classifiers understand OI.

To be classified, you have what's called a "classification appointment." At your appointment, you must perform physical strength and function tests and allow yourself to be observed, measured, and assessed. Classifiers pull on your limbs and might push or twist your body into uncomfortable positions.

This terrifies me. Even when I explain OI, not everyone understands how fragile my body really is. I'm just not comfortable with people touching me who are not well-versed in OI.

In the beginning, it was even hard for me to get classified at all because sometimes, it was determined I wasn't disabled enough to compete. I remember my mother being particularly upset at a meet in Minneapolis, when after my classification appointment, we were told I could swim only breaststroke. The classifiers said my OI and associated traits did not impact me enough to qualify to swim the other strokes.

We were distraught, and we stood in the hallway after getting the news, not sure of our next step. We'd come all that way! For just breaststroke?

This time, yes.

Glenda, who was officiating the meet, saw us, and all she could do was give us a big hug.

There wasn't much else to do. Classifiers' rulings are hard to overturn, and it's not always in your best interest to fight.

Still, "You've got to be an advocate," Coach Fred told my mom. "You live with this and know the most about your child."

Coach Fred believes I might've been the only OI swimmer competing in para meets in those early years. So it makes sense that it took lots of advocacy on my mom's part, and plenty of education (on both sides) before I was classified correctly.

There was at least one other contributing factor to things eventually getting easier on the classification front: as I got older, my disability advanced. This made my needs more obvious to classifiers, but the flip side—becoming more disabled—was and continues to be a heartbreaking trade-off.

CHAPTER THREE

MOM + COACH = MOACH

My mom didn't learn to swim until she was a senior in high school. Her mother, my Bye-Bye, had been deathly afraid of water and would not let my mom go in past her knees.

It seems a little crazy that with that back story, my mom ended up a swim coach, but she did, starting with the Habersham Rapids.

"All the fun stuff, that was Teresa," Coach Anthony remembers. "I was the nuts-and-bolts guy, and Teresa was behind the scenes making it memorable for everybody."

My mom learned from Coach Anthony, but she also spent a lot of time educating herself with American Swim Coaches Association classes and by watching videos. "She was a very deliberate student of the sport," Coach Anthony says.

She also was working nights as a respiratory therapist. Add in homeschooling and all the time we spent going to physical therapy and other appointments, and I'm not sure she ever slept.

Homeschooling came about unexpectedly. Grant had been attending a private school that required entrance testing, so when it came time for me to go to school, I had an appointment with the admissions department.

My meeting lasted only a short time, which surprised my mom since she remembered what it was like for my brothers. Eli had already been accepted to the school, as well.

"She's done? So soon?" my mom remembers asking.

I hadn't tested well, she was told, and I wasn't ready for school.

"Really?" my mom asked. "What did she miss?"

"McKenzie doesn't know the difference between a violin and a fiddle."

My mom wasn't having it. She pulled Grant, and we became homeschoolers.

That was the first real discrimination I had faced, and I misunderstood it at the time. I thought we were homeschooling because I was in a wheelchair. My mom corrected my misconception by finding a small Christian school in South Carolina that would take all three of us, but after only a year, that school proved not to be a great fit, either.

Eli and I were homeschooled the rest of the time. Grant later attended a private boarding school as a day student where Mom became the swim coach.

It's weird how things work out. My mom having that coaching job at Rabun Gap-Nacoochee School unlocked opportunity for all of us.

I had swum in my first para meet as an 8-year-old in 2005. It was at Georgia Tech in Atlanta, in the same pool that hosted the 1996 Paralympics. At that meet, I met Curtis Lovejoy, who went on to be a five-time Paralympian. He and another Paralympian, Jessica Long, spoke after the meet about their achievements. They talked about how they practiced six or seven days a week.

I was mesmerized. "I want to do that," I told my mom. So we did.

A mere three years later, I qualified for the 2008 Paralympic Trials. I was with my Habersham Rapids friends at the Hollywood

Diner, where we'd hang out while our parents held swim team board meetings, when Coach Fred called with the news. The time standards had been released, and I was fast enough to go. We celebrated loudly, along with everyone else in the restaurant.

At 11 years old, I was the youngest swimmer in the country to qualify. I would swim the 400- and 100-meter freestyles, the 100-meter butterfly, and the 100 back, all as an S9 at the Trials in Minneapolis.

In the end, my highest finish was fifth in the backstroke. It wasn't good enough for a trip to Beijing, but the experience lit a fire in me. My hard work was paying off, and it was time to step it up a notch.

So we decided to leave the Habersham Rapids.

"It happens," Coach Anthony says now. "I understand. We're a small, rural Georgia club. When people start tasting success, there's no holding them back."

Eli and Grant were swimming fast, too. Grant was setting school records at RGNS, and Eli was winning practically every 50 freestyle he swam, even the ones he nearly missed because he was playing his Nintendo DS. The time had come to find a team that attended bigger meets and had more kids to challenge us.

It's still hard to talk about what happened next.

We joined a powerhouse team that practiced more than a half-hour from our house. In a lot of ways, it was what we were looking for—a serious, goal-oriented program with a demanding coach. But the expectations proved unrealistic, especially when it came to me. When I could not keep up with the able-bodied swimmers, not for lack of trying, but simply because my body couldn't do what was being asked, the whole group would be penalized. It was awful.

The coach was rough on Grant, too, bumping him down a group because we would be late for practice because of my mom's job at

Rabun Gap-Nacoochee. Eli, probably because he's so lightning-quick, got off scot-free. But the joy we all knew from swimming evaporated.

Soon after Grant got demoted, he came to practice one day and shook the coach's hand.

"I really appreciate everything you've done for me," he said, "but I have to respectfully decline your decision. We'll be leaving now."

And that's how Mom became our coach.

We affectionately called her "Moach."

Having keys to the RGNS pool came in handy. Eli and I became training partners, using the pool when Grant and his Rabun Gap team were not.

Our workouts were difficult, and if I did not swim a set as perfectly as I wanted to, I tended to beat myself up. That made things both easy and hard for my mom. She didn't have to correct me much—I was usually way ahead of her. But she had to remind me to leave those disappointments in the pool.

We all had to work at keeping things separate. School time was for learning; pool time was for swimming; car time was for fighting over the radio (but not the front seat—Grant always got the front seat); and down time was for Dad.

My dad is a lifelong Clemson University football fan. He grew up near the South Carolina school, and even he jokingly calls his devotion to its football team "a disease." When Grant was born, he started taking him to games, and later, he took Eli, too, who, unsurprisingly, thrived in the noise and chaos of game day more than any of them.

But what about me? Getting in and out of a football stadium with 80,000 oblivious people just wasn't a good idea. I so badly wanted to go, though, so Dad started taking me to Clemson basketball, instead.

My dad's sister had season tickets. Her pair of seats were on the lower level, in the first row off the mezzanine, right on the edge. I was able to park my wheelchair and take only one step to get into my spot. I felt safe and comfortable, and I began to really enjoy basketball, especially because it meant spending time with my dad. Before long, I considered myself a true fan, enough that if I weren't a swimmer, my second-choice sport would be wheelchair basketball. (Not realistic, of course—it's way too rough, but it's awesome to watch!)

My parents made sure we had enough time for family vacations, too, and cruising was something we all enjoyed. The ships were amazingly accessible with elevators everywhere. Eli, Grant, and I were given a lot of freedom whenever we were on a cruise. I mean, how far could we go?

My dad and I shared one other special activity—the Valentine's Day daddy-daughter dances at the Gainesville Civic Center, about 40 minutes from Clarkesville. We went for six or seven years, joined by several other friends/father-daughter pairs.

To dance with my dad both in my wheelchair and out was good for both of us. While my mom and I saw my wheelchair as way for me to be more independent, my dad, at first, had seen it as a stark reminder of the gravity of my disability.

"It made me realize," he says now, "that this is for life."

Those Valentine dances showed him another side of wheelchair living. "They were a lot of fun," my dad remembers. "It was just a laid-back evening, a perfect evening together."

Time to relax was brief and scattered, though. Swimming was becoming more serious. Mom had taken over coaching us, I'd been to a Paralympic Trials meet, and my swimming career was taking off.

But, at 13 years old, I still didn't know how to do a racing dive from a starting block.

I'd been taught a dive progression when I was little—sit on the edge, arms in a streamline arrow above my head, tuck my chin, and slide in like a knife. Then do the same thing kneeling, then standing, bending over to gently slide my fingers, then arms, head, and the rest of my body into the water.

But from a starting block? Never. So far, in most of my races, I had started in the water, pushing off the wall. Sometimes, including at the Trials for Beijing, I started with a cautious dive from the side. Both ways were slower than diving from the block, which allows a powerful launch through the air, taking advantage of less resistance than through water.

At able-bodied meets, my in-water start slowed down the meet and was cause for more eyes on me than I cared for. But starting from a push meant I didn't have to worry about belly-flopping at full speed from a height of 18 to 30 inches above the surface. I didn't have to worry about breaking anything.

A racing start, though, would make me more competitive on the national and international level, and that was my goal. So one time at the Gainesville YMCA, we were, like, "Let's try it."

And then, "Oh, God."

It was so high up there.

Worst-case scenarios rushed my brain in waves of adrenaline.

Just do what you do from the side, I coached myself. *You can't hit it flat. You have to go in at an angle, McKenzie, just like off the side.*

"Take your mark," my mother said.

I quickly shushed the noise in my head, and at her whistle I dove off the block through a tunnel in my mind.

It took me a moment to realize, *Oh, I'm underwater! Oh, I'm fine.*

Fine! Everyone watching could exhale.

In that last instant, I had drilled down on what needed to happen—hear the start, jump, and swing my arms forward, slice the surface of the water with my fingers, and dive through the hole. Streamline, kick, and break out fast!

There was no room for error, so I hadn't allowed it.

When I imagine a desired outcome, it's more likely to come true. By training my brain on success, my body then follows the expectation. To this day, I rely on my ability to laser-focus before racing and other challenging situations.

I developed this skill in the hospital. Staying calm and focusing my thoughts elsewhere helped me to get through painful procedures. Sometimes, I would think about swimming to overcome fear when I was being rolled into an operating room.

Later in my swim career, I gained a reputation for my fearsome, pre-race facial expressions.

"You're absolutely terrifying in the call room," a swim friend once told me. "You give these looks that make me want to crawl in a ball and die!"

The call room is the place at a major meet where swimmers wait for their heat to be announced. The call room is always thick with intensity, but people are often surprised at the juxtaposition between my usual giggly-fun self and the focus I turn on before a race.

When it comes down to the wire, I can go into my own little world and shut people out, and just do what needs to be done. I might look murderous in the moment, but I'm happy with it. Seriously.

I've also developed a "no regrets" philosophy. It is harder for me to not know whether I can do something than it is for me to not try. What's the worst that can happen? A trip to the ER? Been there, done that. No, the worst thing is to not try.

That day at the Y, after the unexpected and fleeting surge of self-doubt, I was confident in my ability. I knew the risks of diving from that height, but where would I be now if I hadn't done it, anyway? If I hadn't continued to do it in all my important races?

Years earlier, I had approached flip turns similarly. Flip turns, done correctly, save time on each wall of a race. They allow you to somersault to change direction, and push off the wall with your feet, instead of swimming into the wall, touching with your hand, pivoting your body, and then pushing off. My physical therapist was against flip turns, worried that the momentum would be too much for the bones in my feet.

I already had broken many fingers, for instance, at the end of races when I finished with some speed behind me.

But, really, what's a toe? An ankle? I knew I could handle that because I'd already handled much more.

I started sneaking flip turns in practice. I'd sometimes pop up, look over at my mom, and see her wagging her finger. I'd hear about it on the drive home, too, my mom breaking her "leave it at the pool" rule.

"If you want to continue swimming, we need to be able to trust you to make safe decisions for yourself," she'd say.

I'd roll my eyes.

I really had no interest in living my life like a China doll.

Increasingly, I found myself among the elite of Paralympic swimmers, and I was loving it. I was set on making the 2012 London Games team. One thing that would help make that possible was wearing a tech suit in competition.

Tech suits are ultra-tight swimsuits that improve hydrodynamics. Swimmers wear them a couple of sizes smaller than what is comfortable to flatten body bulges, wrinkles, and curves. Wearing a tech suit is a rite of passage for swimmers—it means you've reached a level of swimming where the tiniest of advantages count.

I wore my first tech suit, a gift from my parents, at the Beijing Trials. It was sleek and cut like a regular one-piece swimsuit. Many of my competitors wore knee-length or full-body suits, but I was only 11—there wasn't much to me at that age that needed squeezing and compressing. Still, the suit made me feel like a big shot, and I looked like one, too. That confidence boost was priceless.

Soon, though, it was clear that a knee-length tech suit was what I needed. This presented a few challenges.

Putting on a tech suit is a workout in itself for anyone. The suit is literally too small, and it has sticky grips inside, so you must contort your body and stretch the suit over your skin. This has to be done ever-so gingerly because the fancy fabric the suit is made of is actually quite fragile, so rips are common and can really ruin your day.

A tech suit can cost many hundreds of dollars. A torn tech suit is worth nothing.

It takes 15-20 minutes for an able-bodied swimmer to put on a tech suit. Once it's on, the straps dig into the tops of your shoulders, so this, plus the fact it's so delicate, means a tech suit is generally worn for only a short time, maybe just for finals at a championship-format meet. Every time it's worn, too, the material's elasticity degrades a bit, so the suit might only be used for a few meets, or less, if you're swimming at the highest levels.

When I started wearing a tech suit, we needed a plan. How was the girl for whom newborn onesies were once too complicated going to shove herself into a tech suit?

Turns out, it takes 30 minutes, three people, a plastic bag, a towel, and a bottle of Lysol to get it done.

I found that laying down works the best, and usually that means on a locker room floor. Hence, the Lysol and towel.

Then, I need two people who I trust implicitly and who will tolerate my nerviness, to help pull on the suit. We use a plastic bag to cover the body part we're working on, to provide a little bit of slip, and then once that part of the suit is on, we pull out the bag, smooth the suit, and move the bag to the next location.

It's a patient, choreographed, almost artful process, and I'll put the fear of God into anyone helping me.

"Do not grab me. Do not twist me. Do not pull me."

Then, I'll anxiously plead to myself, *Please, don't rip. Please, don't pop.*

But, yes, I have torn a suit, and yes, I have heard a shoulder pop, fracturing under the pressure of a strap.

I'm not going to lie. Putting on a tech suit as a person with OI is more nerve-wracking than racing, and once it's on, the relief and satisfaction often are more than what I feel when I touch the wall in first place.

In March 2010, I knew I had a realistic shot at making the team for the 2012 Paralympic Games in London.

I had had an epic 400-meter freestyle at the U.S. Paralympic Spring Swimming Nationals in San Antonio. People were approaching me, congratulating me, and it hit me: I was in the mix! It was starting to become very real.

More than ever, I focused on swimming and making the Paralympic Team. I was definitely not doing the regular teenager things. I mean, I had friends, but I was not interested in boys or going out. That just wasn't me. I wanted London.

My mom spent a lot of time watching the international rankings, which are a key component to making the Paralympic Team. For Paralympians, making the team is as much how fast you swim as it is how you compare to other swimmers around the world in your classification. This is different from making the Olympic swim team, which is named from the top two swimmers in each event at the Olympic Trials meet.

At the Paralympic Trials, you might get second in your best event, and still not make the Paralympic Team, because your international ranking isn't high enough. Or you might touch third and get a spot. The national governing body announces the team the day after the meet is over. It's a tricky system, so you have to know where you stand, or the suspense can be awful.

During the time heading into London, I was classed as an S9, so my mom studied the S7s, S8s, and S10s, too, in case my or anyone else's classification changed. She made a spreadsheet to keep track of people's times, and she watched videos of my competition whenever they were available.

What's their stroke rate? she'd wonder. *How fast do they get off the wall? Where's their breakout?*

We can't beat them here, she'd think, maybe noticing their start. *But we can get them here,* eyeing a weakness.

My mom didn't worry me with these details. She would just adjust my workouts to build my strength and skills where they could be the most effective. My arms are long, for instance, so my distance per stroke is A-plus. We did a lot of stroke-rate work to get the most out of my arms. Also, we knew that I'd likely never out-dive someone, but I could out-swim anyone, so we focused on longer events where I had more distance to catch people and overtake them.

My job, Moach would tell me, was to learn to be calm, to follow the plan, to trust her.

In February 2012, I had a classification appointment at a meet in Colorado Springs. I knew I had progressed in my disability, which is not good, but I was glad to be reclassified in a way that made things more fair.

Starting at that meet, I would compete as an S8, and I made the U.S. Paralympic National Team for the first time. Both were a big deal. Being an S8 just felt right. It was where I belonged. And earning my place on the national team, realizing I belonged there, too, was thrilling. I had looked up to national team members for years. There was a specialness about them—the way they carried themselves on deck was so professional and respectful, and I had strived to copy their example.

Now, I was one of them, and four short months later, I was headed to Bismarck State College in North Dakota for the U.S. Paralympic Swimming Trials.

The meet started on my 16th birthday, and my best event, the 400-meter freestyle, was on the first day.

My mom thinks that it being my birthday messed with my head. Who knows? She might be right, but the thing I'm sure of is that I woke up that morning feeling petrified. Normally, I have the good kind of nerves before I swim. But that day—maybe because things had gone so well up to that point—I was a mess, like I was expecting bad news.

In warmup, I couldn't find my rhythm, swimming way too fast on my pace 50s. There was no way I could hold that speed over the course of a 400.

My head was filled with worries. I was overly critical of myself and couldn't focus on the one thing I needed to do: swim.

"Get it together," my mom said. "You're fine. Relax."

But I couldn't relax, and I wasn't fine. I had a horrible swim in my preliminary heat of the 400 free, adding a couple of seconds to my seed time. Even though I qualified third for the final, it was going to take so much more to make the team, considering world rankings.

I felt deflated. This was my real shot, and it was just not happening.

It was time for some tough love.

"This is ridiculous," my mom said. "You are not going to throw away everything you've done up to now. I'm not having it."

And that's all she said. What was the point in talking, anyway? I was too upset for any reason to get through to me. Mom got me some lunch, and we drove back to the hotel silently. She turned on the A/C in the room, turned off the lights, and left.

I don't remember sleeping. I do recall sitting there, staring at the wall.

You can't swim scared, I told myself. *Scared has never worked for you.*

Go into your bubble and focus.

When it was time to go back for finals, my mom still didn't speak to me. Warmup went well. Before I went to the call room, my mom's message to me was simple: "You got this."

I hardly remember that swim.

What I know was that I touched the wall in second place behind Jessica Long, who set a world record. I was a mere .11 seconds ahead of the third swimmer, Brickelle Bro. Brickelle and I had been rivals for a while, and I knew as soon as I saw the scoreboard we were likely to be teammates soon. My time was good for fourth in the world. It should be good enough to punch my ticket to London.

I looked into the stands. My dad and brothers were cheering like crazy. My mom was bawling.

I was crying, too. I could hardly contain myself. *Did this just happen?* I thought. *In Bismarck, North Dakota?*

That night, the whole family went to dinner. I remember the wait staff bringing out a birthday cake and singing to me, and it felt like the greatest moment of my life.

My spot on the London team would be confirmed three days later, after two more days of strong swimming and a long, tortured night of second-guessing after the meet was over.

It really is exhausting not knowing if you made the team for sure, on the spot, after you swim. That last night in Bismarck, I found myself repeating, *Please, take me. Please, take me,* in my head, and then waiting, sleepless. I couldn't rest until the announcement was made.

The morning after the meet, all the swimmers were gathered in an auditorium on the Bismarck State College campus. I sat next to my mom and Grant. Dad and Eli had flown home already.

My nails dug into my mom's hand as she held mine through a hype video that showed all the sites and venues in London. I couldn't help but question the timing—some of us would soon be learning we had not been picked for the trip. It seemed mean to pump everyone up, only to know some of us would be let down.

One of the national team staff clicked off the video. "And now we'd like to announce the 2012 U.S. Paralympic Swim Team!"

Names were called in alphabetical order, and swimmers were handed a folder that said something like "2012 Team USA" on it. I heard them get to the "Cs," and then I kind of blanked. They called me, and I did nothing. I just sat there.

"Um, McKenzie?" the staff person handing out the folders said. "That's you!"

Cue the hugs and tears, all over again.

It had been 16 years since my mother had given birth to me, a child who many thought wouldn't live at all, let alone live well.

My mom had always said to anyone who doubted, "Don't underestimate McKenzie."

And to me when the doubters got me down, she'd say, "They don't know you. They don't know how strong you are."

As usual, she was right, but I doubt even Moach could imagine a better way for us to celebrate my 16th birthday, which will be forever remembered for its gifts: confidence, strength, elation, and a ticket to London!

CHAPTER FOUR

LONDON

There was plenty of work to be done in the two months before leaving for London, plus a little celebrating.

I was swimming—and coaching little kids, too—that summer with a new team my mom had started just a few months prior at the Cumming Aquatic Center, about an hour from our house. When I walked into the Waves' workout the day after returning from Trials and saw all the signs and cheering, I was overwhelmed in the best possible way.

I appreciated it for a minute, but I couldn't help but feel like the attention was a bit much. "We don't need to do all this," I said. "Let's get to practice."

The CAC was a brand-new, indoor facility that was set up long course, which is how the Paralympic pool would be configured. My workouts with the senior-level group were intense, and at the end of each one, I would swim 16, 50-meter freestyles on a 1-minute interval. The idea was to hold my 400-meter goal pace, so I wanted to touch the wall for each 50 in 39-40 seconds, and then get 20-21 seconds of rest.

I did this set alone and exhausted, and that was the point. A 400-meter freestyle is only eight 50s, but by my swimming double that at race pace every day, I would train both my body and mind to grind out that speed and confidently know I could hold it for twice longer than what was needed.

We hoped by doing this, I'd forever avoid the nasty jitters I'd had during prelims at Trials.

In July, the Paralympic Team traveled to the Speedo Can/Am Para Swimming Championships in Winnipeg, Canada. It was a fairly low-key meet, mostly a chance for the coaches to see how our training was going at home and for the swimmers to gel as a team before heading to the Games.

It also was my first trip without my mom.

The day I left, Curtis Lovejoy, whom I had looked up to since my first para meet at Georgia Tech as an 8-year-old, was at my airport gate. He couldn't help but laugh, watching my mom and me saying good-bye and trying to hold back tears.

"The first one is always the hardest," I remember him saying.

I hugged my mom like I never had before and then boarded the plane. We both knew it was the beginning of a whole new ballgame.

It's hard to imagine a better time in my life than when I was handed that official team folder in Bismarck. But on the Winnipeg trip, my good fortune started sinking in as I got to know my teammates, especially Colleen Young, a 14-year-old from St. Louis, who would quickly become my best friend.

I had first noticed Colleen at the March 2010 Nationals in San Antonio. I'd never seen a person with albinism before, and I couldn't help but be fascinated. I tried to talk to her in the warm-down pool, but I nervously stuttered and squeaked, and she didn't even realize I was trying to say "hi." She just pushed off the wall and swam away.

She'd made an impression on me again in Bismarck, after they announced the London team. At lunch that day, Colleen broke a tense silence at the rookie table with an out-of-the-blue snort and laugh.

Yeah, I'm gonna like her, I remember thinking.

In Winnipeg, Colleen and I were assigned the same car to and from the pool. A coach drove. I was the front-seat navigator, and Colleen was the back-seat singer. After three days of Colleen rapping to Pitbull's "International Love," our coach, Peggy, snapped off the music.

"I can't take it, anymore!" she yelled, and we drove around Canada in the quietest car ever, from that point on.

Colleen and I were among a handful of teenagers on the Paralympic team. We tried hard to fit in and act like we knew what we were doing, but we were mostly faking it. There are a lot of unspoken rules of behavior when you represent Team USA, and we did our best to not earn any side eyes, arched eyebrows, or coach exasperation. But that's hard when you're prone to bursting out in song.

The Games would start at the end of August, a little more than a month after Winnipeg. Before we were to be in London, the team would go to Stuttgart, Germany, for a two-week training camp.

For that part of the trip, Colleen and I had adjoining rooms in a haunted hotel.

OK, maybe not haunted, but how else do you explain the toilet flushing on its own at random times? The hotel was on top of a huge hill on a converted military base. The place gave us both the creeps, so we kept our common door open, built a pillow fort down the middle of one of the gigantic beds, and slept together to keep each other company.

Between two-a-day swim workouts and weightlifting, we'd watch reality TV, and we even crafted what we thought was an excellent pitch for a show about Paralympians and all the behind-the-team drama to the TLC network. (They love disabled people, right?) We'd pass more time doing makeovers. I used a CoverGirl eyeshadow palette with neon colors on Colleen—you know, so we'd be inconspicuous when we snuck out for Pizza Hut breadsticks.

We stuck together. We missed our families, and we would have done anything to have someone familiar there with us. At the same time, our friendship was growing into a sisterhood I'd come to love.

One night not long into camp, I heard a scream to wake the dead and a loud thump from Colleen's side of the pass-through.

Oh, that can't be good, I thought.

I found Colleen on the ground.

"Are you OK?" I asked in a panic.

She pointed to her right foot, where her middle toe was swelling and turning purple. She'd kicked an errant suitcase and went down hard.

"Dude! I think you broke your toe!" I cried.

To myself, I thought, *This is OK. Thank God. It's just a toe.*

I knew it hurt, though. I could almost feel it myself. But neither of us wanted to alert the medical staff. It was late, and we were afraid of getting in trouble. Certainly, I had enough broken-bone experience to help fix a smashed toe.

We needed ice. *Where's ice?*

Still dressed in our pajamas, I helped Colleen hop-wimper downstairs to the team room.

"Shhhh!" I'd say, trying to comfort and, at the same time, take charge of the situation. "We don't want anyone to know we're up!"

We slipped our key card through the lock of the team room. We'd made it, undetected. But when we opened the door, we saw all the older swimmers in there, hanging out together.

Heads turned, like on swivels, to stare at us.

So much for keeping "Operation Find Ice" a secret.

"She broke her toe!" I exclaimed, and we giggled like, well, girls. We were so embarrassed, standing there in our bed clothes. I did a walk of shame across the room to get a bag of ice, and we hightailed it out of there, as fast as Colleen could limp.

Colleen adapted quickly to life with nine good toes, and the whole ordeal wasn't even the most unexpected thing to happen when we were in Germany.

Even more surprising? We never heard back from TLC.

There was at least one more, much more significant surprise when we got to London.

I was slated to swim three events, the 400-meter free, 100 backstroke, and 200 individual medley. But in a last-minute change brought on by a teammate's reclassification, I got bumped from the backstroke and IM.

Mallory Weggemann was reclassified at the Games to become an S8. The rejiggered lineup left me out of the back and IM because I was no longer among the fastest three on the team in those events. This was disappointing, of course, but it was no doubt worse for Mallory, who had been favored to win multiple golds as an S7.

Mallory went on to win the S8 50 free, thank goodness. And the rule allowing reclassification at a Paralympic Games has since been changed, giving all of us peace of mind for the future. At the time in

London, though, being caught in the ripples of such a decision was a tough learning experience. I had no choice but to make the most of what I had left on my program, and I was thankful it was my favorite event, the 400 free.

Being grateful didn't erase the nerves, though. The morning of my race, I teared up in the locker room while talking to one of the coaches and Jessica Long. I hated that I cried, which only compounded my distress. I didn't want my inexperience to show in front of a staff member and a bajillion-times gold medalist.

They were kind, though, and they calmed me, assuring me that I belonged there and I wouldn't let down the team or my family. Afterward, I talked to both my parents, and overall, I felt better. It was time to race.

My preliminary swim for the 400 was my best ever. I dropped 10 seconds off my time and was seeded fourth with a 5:17.94 for the final that evening. Jessica, who already held the world and Paralympic Games records in the event, was the top seed. Brickelle Bro rounded out the field so Team USA had three of the eight swimmers in the final.

I smiled the whole bus ride back to the Olympic Village, where I rested until finals.

Every finals heat comes with a bit of a show. It makes for good TV and gets the crowd excited. Each swimmer's name and country are announced as we leave the call room to go to our blocks, one-by-one, and there's lots of cheering after each name.

I barely noticed the hoopla, though, as I rolled to Lane 6, goggles on my eyes before I even got to my block.

A series of quick, short whistles signaled us to get ready, and a longer whistle called for the spectators' silence. Then, a familiar voice:

"Take your mark."

It was Glenda!

Glenda was one of the meet starters, and by chance, she was assigned to the women's races that night. For the smallest of instants on that international stage, my focus was interrupted by a comforting sound from home.

As an official, Glenda isn't allowed to cheer or show favoritism.

"I was biting the inside of my lip," she says now, "and my heart was beating fast. It was just so awesome."

I have to agree.

Jessica dominated that night, smashing her own world record with a 4:42.28.

I finished sixth, adding a bit to my morning swim after going out too fast, touching in 5:20.57. Brickelle was fifth, a mere tenth of a second quicker.

I was so proud to have represented my country, and to have made the final was a humbling honor.

But to be finished so early in the Games was bittersweet. Some days, I struggled to fit in, and I had trouble sleeping. When I woke up, I felt anxious until I remembered I was done competing. I still swam every day, taking advantage of access to excellent coaches, but my workouts were up and down. I found I had much to learn about swimming, which was weird, I thought, because there I was, already a Paralympian. I should have all the tools and answers, right? Nope. Surrounded by so many world-class athletes, I felt brand-new to the sport.

I found plenty of positives, though, to having so much extra time. I threw myself into supporting my teammates and cheering for every swim. Colleen made the S13 finals twice—she ended up fifth in the 100 breaststroke and seventh in the 200 IM. I relished collecting and trading the commemorative country pins, which are traditional Olympic and Paralympic souvenirs. I even got a coveted, limited-edition koala pin from one of the Australians.

If pin trading were a sport, I know I'd win the gold.

Nearly two weeks after it all began, I cried as we marched into the Closing Ceremonies. It was such an overwhelming mix of emotions! I had fulfilled a dream, but it had been so draining. I was glad it was over, but I knew I'd soon miss all my new friends and coaches. I set it all aside to enjoy the incredible night of music and dancing.

Coldplay, the British Paraorchestra, Jay-Z, and my all-time favorite, Rihanna, performed.

Rihanna flew around on a giant swing, singing "We Found Love," and at one point, she was directly above me.

I held my phone out to record it, and, I promise, I saw her wink at me.

A few non-swimming memories stand out when I think back on the London Paralympics—first impressions of the Olympic Village, for instance, and the wardrobe extravaganza called "team processing."

We flew from Stuttgart to London in a private plane, which should have been my clue that we were in for some special treatment. When we arrived, porters grabbed our luggage, we were issued credentials, and we boarded buses that had tinted windows, but that didn't stop people on the streets from trying to take our pictures.

Getting into the Village was like airport security but stricter, and once we were inside, it was as if we'd entered our own little country. There were shops and apartments, massage spas and beauty salons, a minimart, and more than one hospital. The cafeteria had every world cuisine you could ever want to try, including McDonald's, which I craved the most. (We'd just suffered through two weeks of haunted hotel German food, after all.)

I could live here forever, I remember thinking.

Each of us was given a blanket that said "London 2012," and it had all the logos from the different sports. It was a thoughtful gift and useful for the dorms.

Our rooms in Team USA House were suitable. I bunked with Mallory Weggemann and another swimmer. My single bed was sandwiched between theirs, and while that was a little awkward, I didn't mind. I was so happy to be there, I would have slept on the sidewalk.

Uniforms and apparel came on the second day we were in London, during team processing. We were told the experience was going to be amazing, and nothing could have been truer.

We were taken to a warehouse that was set up like a mall with shops from the Games' sponsors. Everything inside was free, and we were expected to visit as many booths as we could.

I was assigned a personal handler who would find and trade clothing sizes, and who would carry my bags and bring me water and snacks. At times, I felt guilty about the attention, especially when I was fitted by a tailor for my Opening and Closing Ceremonies outfits. It was all a little too much—four hours and four, full suitcases too much—but don't get me wrong, I let myself enjoy it.

The marketing slogan for the London Paralympic Games was "Inspire a Generation," and its message went far beyond the pool and playing fields. Muscular, strong para athletes were featured on billboards and on sides of buses, and fans filled venues to capacity.

In my 400 free, the swimmer next to me in Lane 5 was from Great Britain. When she was introduced, the crowd noise was incredible, and later, when I was a spectator, I can tell you, when a Team GB swimmer was competing, the stadium-style seating roared and shook.

The London Games is credited with being the first Paralympics promoted as an event for elite-level athletes, focused on abilities rather than impairments. Research since shows it made a significant contribution toward change and opportunity for disabled people in the United Kingdom. Attitudes and perceptions improved toward disabled people, and a 2018 government study revealed that nearly a million more people with disabilities were employed in Great Britain then, compared to a year after the Games.

Every Paralympics aspires to leave a lasting impact on the community in which it is held. Knowing the London Games bettered the lives of others and inspired the minds of still more, makes me even prouder to have been there.

After London, I lived on a high for a while. People in town recognized me and wanted to talk to me, and I loved that. I was starting to think about college, as well, and all the excitement that comes with deciding where to go.

There was post-Games stress, too. It was hard to be a normal teenager after having had such an awesome experience like the Paralympics. It's not like there was anyone else in Clarkesville, Georgia, who had any idea what I'd experienced. And while my new goal was to make the next Paralympics, I now felt an expectation that I would. The external pressure, imagined or not, added to the demands I already put on myself, and it was a little suffocating.

My workouts with the Waves were geared toward the next big meet, the 2013 World Championships, which would be held in

August in Montreal, Canada. It would be the first international competition for the national team since London, and I was anxious to swim and see my teammates. The trials for it were in Minneapolis in April.

I don't know what happened in Minneapolis. Everything was off.

It was two weeks after the trials before the World Championships roster was set, and the texts started flying about an hour prior to the official list being published.

"Did you get an email?" swimmer friends were asking. "I got mine."

Mine never came.

I can't remember how many swimmers were picked—20 or maybe 22? All I know is that I was either number 21 or 23 when the list was made public. I wasn't going to Montreal.

It was a terrible feeling.

What would people think? I worried. *Was I only a one-hit wonder? I hadn't even medaled in London! What if I never had another chance?*

I stayed off the internet and social media and could hardly stand to think about not making the team. It was a rough time, and at nearly 17, I felt like I had failed at life.

That's a big reaction to not being picked for a team. But I had had so much recent success that my perspective was as off as my performance, and it felt like my world's bottom had fallen out.

I wanted to never feel that way again.

CHAPTER FIVE

LIVING WITH OI

Setbacks can be motivating, and I was determined to come back from missing World Championships even stronger than before.

I'd rebounded from more difficult things, after all. By the time I swam in London, I'd had countless broken bones (really, at some point, we stopped keeping track), and several major surgeries to repair them. Each of these injuries required either the fortitude to keep swimming or the wisdom to wait.

Waiting is always harder for me. I hate being sidetracked from a goal, so when I am injured, the pain of the break is often less than the anguish of the imposed detour. Perhaps the only exception is for a broken femur, which is both excruciatingly painful and the slowest to heal. It's a double-whammy injury.

While growing up, my right femur was weaker than my left, and once a bone is broken, it is more vulnerable to breaking again. It was my right leg that had had the spiral fracture when I tried to run with my walker, and it was my right femur that I broke again when I was 3, probably playing with Eli. That time, I ended up in two separate body casts.

The first was on for four weeks to stabilize me before having surgery to repair the fracture. I wore the post-op body cast for an additional six weeks.

When you wake up from a surgery in a body cast, it feels like the walls are closing in on you, or like someone is on top of you, or you're in a closed box, and you can't get out.

A body cast covers from ankles to armpits. It puts you in a mostly lying-down position for what can be months. You literally can't move—can't sit, can't walk around. It constricts your torso, which is a particular problem for me and my barrel chest. When I'm in a body cast, I can't get a full breath.

Whenever I was casted like that, my mom would help by moving me onto my side, to give my lungs a break from being in such a weird position and maybe help get me more oxygen. That wasn't enough, though, to keep the experience from contributing to claustrophobia and heightened anxiety in everyday life.

I don't like being in crowds, for instance, especially when I'm in my wheelchair. I'm so much shorter, and it feels like everyone is on top of me. I get that same "I can't breathe. I have to get out" feeling that I do when I'm in a body cast.

I don't look straight ahead when I walk because I live in a constant state of worry over potential slips and falls. I scan the ground, looking for wet floors, cracks in concrete and other potential dangers. When I'm in a body cast, and I can't get around at all, the anxiety is amplified.

I seriously can't get out of here, I'll think. And then I'll panic.

What if there's an emergency?

What if there's a house fire?

People don't always realize the psychological effects of having a condition like OI and its associated treatments, but they are very real and oftentimes very scary. Yet in many ways, they made me stronger.

Everything is temporary, I'll tell myself in my most shallow-breathed moments. *You can get through this.*

I also still use the strategy my mom learned from her OI mentor-mom, Juanita. When I am hurt or suffer other disappointment, I'll give myself a day or two to be emotional about it. Then, it's time to suck it up and push through. This doesn't mean I bury my feelings. I don't, and my mom never asked me to. But I do not let my emotions overcome me beyond a couple of days.

If I spent two months wallowing every time I was in a body cast, I can't imagine where I'd be today.

Being laid up in a body cast and world-class athletic performance are on opposite ends of the spectrum of physical health and activity. But in my case, they are closely connected. Without the agony and suffering of one, I doubt I'd know or appreciate as much the victory and joy of the other.

Coming to grips with what I must do differently than most people has been a lifelong learning process. I've made plenty of mistakes that in hindsight seem like they could have been avoided.

Like, I shouldn't wear socks in the house. In 2004, after being warned repeatedly to put on shoes, or at least to take off my socks, I slipped at home and broke my right femur, again.

Then, when I was maneuvering into the minivan to go to the hospital, I had a quick thought: *Gosh, that's a lot of pressure on my shoulder.* But before I could get the words out and we could change our tactics, I heard a snap. *Oh, crap.*

"It's pretty broken," they said at the hospital, looking at X-rays of my left shoulder.

"Yeah, that's what I figured," I remember saying.

Having two major breaks at the same time was new to us and required creative adjustments and solutions to everyday tasks. There would be no more sitting up in the van, for example. I'd be lying on the floor in the back, now, my mom having held up my leg while I used my right arm to scoot into the best position.

Different bones feel differently when they break. Backs ache. The pelvis burns. Broken arms and shoulders shoot fire through your limb with every accidental twitch. Feet hurt worse at night and keep you awake. Broken femurs, without question, top the pain scale, so I hardly noticed the shoulder break this time.

I get muscle spasms with a leg break, and these can go on for a couple of weeks. The spasms make my entire body tense, and I worry about the tension leading to another fracture. I find myself holding my breath a lot. I also often run a fever with a femur fracture, so I feel sick on top of things.

Only sleep brings real comfort and escape—except when it doesn't. I have a recurring nightmare that frequently comes when I'm dealing with a fracture. I dream that I've fallen off a building, and just before I hit the ground, I bolt awake. The dread of the jarring, shocking jerk can keep me from sleeping at all, putting relief viciously out of reach.

I've been pretty lucky with the bones in my arms. For whatever reason, they seem stronger than the rest of me. In fact, I have only one enduring memory of a broken arm. It was a Saturday, and I must have been 6 or 7 years old. Dad was in charge of Eli and me. Grant was at a friend's house, and Mom was working a respiratory therapy shift.

Dad was in the living room watching football, so Eli and I thought it would be a good idea to play football ourselves. Eli, only 5 but already very competitive, was unhappy after I crawled to a touchdown. It's not like I taunted him with a celebratory dance or anything, but for the record, I should have. Because I really didn't deserve his chucking that Barbie purse at me.

"Oh, no!" I yelled, rolling on the ground, clutching my arm.

"Oh, no!" Eli yelled.

"Oh, no!" Dad yelled. "Are you kidding me?"

Dad got me a pillow and an ice pack, and the three of us just sat on the couch, looking straight ahead in silence, knowing what was coming.

"Oh, no!" Mom yelled when she walked in the door.

"I was only gone for three hours!"

Just a few months after the Beijing Paralympic Trials, when I was 12, I had a checkup with my orthopedist. I was nervous for the appointment because I knew I had grown.

I wanted to grow, of course. I hated being short. Plus, Eli was taller than me, and that was hard to take. But if I had outgrown the rods in my legs, it would mean surgery. I'd already had two rod replacements since they were inserted after the spiral fracture when I was 2 ½. I was hoping to hear at that appointment in 2008, "We have more time."

I didn't get my wish.

The morning of the surgery, after I'd fasted for 24 hours, for some reason, the procedure was delayed. By late afternoon, it looked like nothing was going to happen that day. I was hungry and upset and more than OK with skipping the whole thing. Again, I didn't get my wish, and they wheeled me to the operating room around 5 or 6 p.m.

The procedure was supposed to be straightforward, with one overnight in the hospital. Instead, the surgery lasted hours longer than expected. My right leg was more messed up than anyone realized. Then, there were surgical complications. I lost a lot of blood. I woke up in a body cast in the intensive care unit and would be there a week.

I remember bits of consciousness, monitors beeping and blaring when my heart rate dropped. I was on oxygen and so many drugs that, at one point, they were counterproductive.

I remember Eli, then 10, sleeping curled up in a wagon in the corner of my hospital room. He remembers being scared.

I consider that rod-replacement surgery to be the lowest of lows in my entire life. It's hard for me and any of my family to think back on it. Only one thing makes the memory bearable: Ch-Ch-Chewie, Chewbacca of Georgia.

I'd been begging for a dog, a Yorkshire terrier, to be exact, for two years at that point. I guess it took my almost dying for my parents to finally give in, and two days after I got home from the hospital, on Christmas Day, Chewie was under the tree. Or maybe chewing the tree. It's hard to say. Probably both. He was a puppy.

Chewie is what got us all through that Christmas, and he would be my treasured companion for the next 11 years.

I also spent a lot of time in that recovery period, as I often did, reading and watching movies. I devoured *The Clique*, a book series about middle-school drama, as well as the Harry Potter books.

I also watched the movie *Legally Blonde* on a loop. I saw myself in Elle Woods, the main character, for her blondeness and love of fashion (my extensive purse collection had expanded beyond Barbie bags at that point). She even, like me, had a little dog, not to mention intelligence, passion, and drive.

I can do that, too, I remember thinking, watching her graduate from Harvard Law. *I can change the world.*

From my bed, I researched law school. How long does it take? What do I need to do to get there?

I'm going to guess that most 12-year-olds don't Google about law school requirements. But I had more time for thinking, or, rather, I used my time for thinking more than most kids do. Looking toward the future and thinking about what I wanted to do with my life helped me to cope with some of my darkest days.

Between the 2008 surgery and the London Games, I had a few other significant challenges.

In July of 2009, I broke my foot jumping into the pool. I wasn't paying attention to the depth, and I landed full force on my left foot in four feet of water. I always protect my right leg—it was pulled up—and I thought the water was deeper.

I heard a few cracks.

Well, nothing I can do about that now, I remember thinking, and I finished swim practice before even looking at it. Afterward, I saw it was black and blue.

The foot fracture didn't hurt much, but the Can/Am meet in Edmonton, Alberta, Canada, was coming up, and I would have to tape and unwrap my foot every warmup and competition session. Bandages are not allowed during a race, so this was a hassle.

The foot injury was a lesson for how to deal with a fracture in a major competition setting. The upside? I'd pass that knowledge to Colleen with her broken toe in just a couple of years!

More seriously, in 2011, I started having what I call femur flare-ups. My right leg never completely healed after the 2008 rodding surgery, and I started having debilitating leg pain. A flare-up can feel like a fresh fracture. Sometimes, it happens if I've been walking too much, but it's usually random, and that's what makes it worse than a true break.

Broken bones heal in time. With a flare-up, the pain comes on indiscriminately, and it wears on indefinitely. I can barely stand the uncertainty of it.

The first time I had a flare-up, an X-ray showed that the rod in my leg had come out of place. Doctors had to push it back into the femur, and I'm not going to lie, that was pretty horrifying.

I live with at least a little bit of pain every day. I'm one of those people who can tell the weather by my aches. When I sit, I shift my weight frequently, to alleviate whichever side hurts. Once I switch sides, the pain radiates, and I'll eventually shift back.

I never know, too, when a rod might slip out of place again, especially in my right leg and hip, and I'll have to stop what I'm doing and pop it back into place. A stretch cord comes in handy for this. I'll wrap it around my hips and pull it to the opposite side while also pushing the bump in with my hands. The first time I did this at swim practice in college, I'm pretty sure my coach was about to vomit.

My own pain tolerance, though, is pretty high, and I try to not mention when I'm hurting. People look at me differently when they know I'm uncomfortable, and I know it makes them uncomfortable to witness my discomfort.

I keep my pain quiet for other reasons, too. I don't want my competition to know when I'm injured in case that gives them any sort of mental boost. Plus, as a Paralympic swimmer, I am part of a movement to raise the esteem of disabled athletes. We should be treated and regarded as the serious athletes we are, and I don't want an injury to be interpreted as weakness.

I've felt this way from very early in my swimming career, when I was sometimes on the receiving end of what we in the para-swim world call "the pity clap."

The pity clap is the well-meaning applause at able-bodied swim meets when a disabled swimmer finishes a race, usually dead last and long enough behind the rest of the heat to be noticeable, especially in longer events.

I want to scream, "Do not clap!" every time I hear it. "Treat us like everybody else!"

But that would drive more attention to the differences. Instead, I lead by example, try not to complain, and aspire to lift the image of disabled athletes worldwide. It's my way of earning, respecting, and elevating the parallel playing field.

My mom says, "There is no normal. Everyone has something they deal with." She's right, and my version of "normal" happens to include disability, as it does for millions of others.

So I deal with what each day throws at me. My doctors, my family, Colleen, and Brian Loeffler, who would become my college swim coach at Loyola University in Baltimore, Maryland, have seen my lowest days firsthand, but not many other people have. As independent as I am, I am forever grateful for my trusted circle's support and acceptance.

CHAPTER SIX

LEAVING HOME AND LOVING LOYOLA

When it was time for me to go to college in 2014, it wasn't a question of if, but where? My dad, understandably, had reservations about my being away from home on my own, but I was ready to go, and my mom understood.

Any school I would consider must have a swim team, and it had to be accessible for my wheelchair and me. I also was ready, as much as I loved my hometown and all the people there, to leave behind rural life for a larger city.

We visited a few in-state options, and obstacles like hills and broken concrete sidewalks ruled them out. We widened our search.

What about Loyola?

Loyola University offers para swimming roster spots both on the college team and on a separate club. Brian Loeffler, the head coach, has a reputation for inclusion and excellence that attracts some of the best para swimmers in the world to Baltimore.

Loyola has a respected political science department, too, which would set me up nicely for law school.

There was only one problem: Brian scared me.

Brian had been one of the national team coaches for the London Games, but he was assigned to other swimmers, so I hadn't gotten to know him well. He seemed a man of few words, and my only real impression of him—a lasting one—came from riding in his rental car one day on the 20-minute drive between the haunted hotel and the training pool in Germany, when he took the Autobahn.

"Buckle up," he said, giving a little nod to me in the back seat. "Get ready to race."

We got to the pool first that day—myself white-knuckled and holding my breath—having survived Brian's wild speed and superior stick-shifting. For the record, I like getting to places early, but I steered clear of Brian's car for the rest of the trip.

Fast forward two years, and I found myself sitting in Brian's office at Loyola. My mom and I had toured the school, and I was sold. The campus was mostly accessible, except for a few areas I would hardly need. Plus, it felt contained, insulated, even, from the big city's potential problems, which was a nice compromise for my parents.

But we couldn't get a read on Brian. *Did he want me as part of the program?* It was hard to tell. I had worked out with one of the para swimmers on Brian's club team and had done a massive test set: 100 yards, 40 times, on a 1:40 interval. It was so hard, I thought I was going to die, but I put everything I had into it.

Despite that effort, Brian seemed distant, even a little standoffish.

We came home with doubts. I badly wanted it to work, though, so Mom went to work on Brian.

Buckle up, Brian.

A few phone calls between my mother and Brian later, everyone felt better acquainted and at ease with one another. We visited a second time, to make sure everything clicked.

It did.

I was ready to race.

Leaving Georgia and my family would be bittersweet, of course, and I'd have to say good-bye to dear friends, too.

My friends were mostly all swimmers, mainly the kids on my mom's Waves team. I would miss my lane mate, Kelsey, the most.

Kelsey and Eli were the same age, and Kelsey's mom, Barbara, was part of the Waves' coaching staff. The three of us, plus a boy named Josh who carpooled with Kelsey, spent a lot of time together, not just training but also hanging out while my mom and Barbara either planned or put away each day's activities.

Kelsey would often be cheering me on through the brutal set of 50s I did each practice leading up to London. We went to dinner every Friday after practice, too, while Mom and Barbara had a coaches meeting.

We were together so much, we started calling our friend group the Cobins, a mashup of Coan and Kelsey's last name, Robins.

I swam in a lane with Kelsey, even though she was faster, because she would look out for me. She cared enough to watch her stroke, so we wouldn't slap hands when we passed each other. (Whoever thinks swimming is a noncontact sport has never slammed the back of their hand against a teammate's or caught a fingertip in a plastic lane rope disc.) Kelsey could keep to her side of the lane, so she made a great lane mate…even when she cheated.

Don't get me wrong, she worked hard. But between Kelsey and Eli, it's safe to say that more than a few 50s were skipped. Not that I was counting. It's also fair to say that Kelsey and Eli balanced my rigidity, and I could use a little bit of that.

Sometimes, just the Cobins and Josh would travel to meets in places like Florida. We had a thousand inside jokes and did silly things only we thought were funny, like pretending to be breeching whales at the end of every practice.

"Whaling" drove my mom crazy, which made it more fun for us.

One day, I was coaching a group of young swimmers. My back was to the water, and suddenly, everything went black, and I fell in. I woke up under water, and my leg was hurt.

Kelsey and Barbara rushed with us to the emergency room in Atlanta and stayed all night while we waited for test results. I don't remember the reason I passed out, and I bounced back quickly, but I'll never forget Kelsey and Barbara being there. Their presence meant the world to me, and I realized our families' friendship ran deeper than most.

On Dec. 10, 2012, just a few months after I got home from London, Kelsey's older brother, Kyle, was killed in a car accident. He was 17.

I saw my mom as she got the news, standing on the pool deck, just before practice. She was talking on her phone with a look on her face that I'd never seen before.

"What's wrong? Are you OK?" I asked, and at the same time, I wondered where Kelsey and Barbara were. They were late.

My mom held the phone away from her ear, and I could hear Kelsey's screams.

My mom left practice in the hands of an assistant coach, and she went to the scene of the accident. So much of what happened next is a blur, and many of the details are lost to trauma, sorrow, and grief. At some point, we were all at the Robins' house. Dad came to get me and Eli.

That part made me angry.

I was trying to figure out what Kelsey needed from me, yet my parents were sending me home. I wanted to yell, "Let me stay!"

At the same time, I didn't know what to do for my friend. I felt so helpless.

I found my place soon.

In the days, weeks, and months following Kyle's death, Kelsey wanted normalcy. We picked her up for swim practice, even when most days she didn't want to go. We were quiet, never pushing her to talk. We cried when she needed to, and we played a lot of Guitar Hero and Mario Kart, too.

Mom urged Barbara to keep coaching. She eventually did, even on days she didn't want to.

The following summer, my mom found a swim meet for the Cobins in the Virgin Islands. The people there were so friendly. A girl at the meet invited us to her house, and we took a boat to get there. We then drove to the top of a hill to find her house overlooking the crystal-blue water.

"It's amazing," Kelsey said of the view that stretched in all directions. I loved seeing her drink it all in, a smile and the sun on her face.

We were a long way from northeast Georgia, a long way from the sadness of the past half-year, and it was just what all of us needed.

While I had experienced loss before in the death of my grandparents and an aunt, when Kyle died, it hit me both individually and as Kelsey's closest friend. Empathy on top of personal loss took grief to another level. Emotionally, I grew up a lot.

Kyle's accident stymied me, though, in other ways, including that I put off getting my driver's license. I'd been in Bismarck for my 16th birthday, so I didn't go to the DMV that day. The London Games and the whirlwind afterward delayed things further. Then Kyle died, and any desire I had to get behind the wheel was gone.

Mine was a logical response, but not a practical one. If I intended to go away for college, I'd need to be able to drive, for, if nothing else, visits home. It took some time—several months past my 17th birthday and nearly a year after Kyle's death—to face my fear and finally take my driver's test.

And then, I failed it. I could not parallel park. I ran over the bright orange cones. Twice.

"Do you want to try again?" the testing woman asked me, skepticism in her voice.

"No. No, I do not," I told her, and I drove back to the DMV and parked in a perfectly-good, angled spot.

"I totally failed this, didn't I?" I asked.

She was slow to answer.

"Do you use your wheelchair all the time?" she asked.

"Yeah," I slowly answered, trying to read her mind, hoping that was what she wanted to hear.

"Oh, well, you won't have to parallel park, anyway," she said.

"Right!" I said. Whew! I had answered her correctly. She'd realized I'd have a disabled parking permit.

"I'll give you your license," she said, "if you promise you'll never parallel park again."

Done.

I came to love driving, and one of my new favorite things to do was to put Chewie in the front seat of my car, turn up Lady Gaga on the radio, and meander Georgia back roads with no particular destination.

Before long, though, I pointed my PT Cruiser toward Baltimore and Loyola's Flannery O'Connor dorm, the residence hall with parallel disabled parking spots out front.

I knew my freshman roommate, Alyssa Gialamas, ahead of time because she was another Paralympic swimmer. We'd crossed paths at meets and would be on Loyola's team together. We both used wheelchairs, and we were given an accessible room, but it still needed a few modifications.

My mom helped me to make a list for the university's facilities team: the washer and dryer needed to be swapped—the stackables were too high; the light switches were out of reach when we were seated in our chairs; emergency lighting needed to be installed, in case I couldn't hear a fire alarm; doorknobs weren't easy to use on the heavy doors—could these be improved?

There were other things on the list, too, and I knew I'd have to ask and advocate for myself, mostly, going forward, but there was a learning curve to that. Later, when I was contacted by the Student Development Office and Disability Support Services to make sure I was adjusting well to campus, I brushed off their outreach and assured them I was fine.

Looking back, I could have made my life easier if I'd only gone in for a chat and let them know my struggles.

Truth is, I was stressed out. Being 600 miles from home was hard, on top of having difficult classes and workouts. Living with strangers was a challenge, too, and that wouldn't get easier for a while. Alyssa and I had only swimming in common, so we didn't hang out much. Then in my sophomore year, I lived with one of Loyola's divers, Katie Ray, and a half-dozen other girls in an apartment-like suite.

These other girls skipped classes, played video games in the middle of the day, and, I came to learn, behaved like—*gasp!*—typical college students. I'd never known people before who would just blow things off, and seemingly not be bothered by looming consequences.

I'd been so focused, so driven, and had surrounded myself with like-motivated people for so long, that I was honestly shocked to learn that the stereotypes of the college-party lifestyle were actually true. And while some of it was entertaining, I really wanted no part of anything they were doing. I was way too Type-A to do "typical college student" very well.

I was the girl, after all, who once asked a friend who was going on and on about a boy she liked, if he were really a "good investment of her time."

So I smiled and waved on the way to my room, and made small talk in the kitchen. I kept my tight schedule and my distance.

Over time, I came to appreciate our differences, though, and I stayed with Katie and most of the same group of other girls through my junior year. We got along well enough, and I even stopped occasionally to beat them at Mario Kart.

I felt more immediately at home in the FAC, as Loyola's Fitness and Aquatics Center is known. I was proud to be part of an esteemed group of Loyola swimmers, a team made up of close to 80 men and women.

Cortney Jordan, a top-ranked 400-meter freestyler who had medaled in the S7 event in London, was part of Loyola's club program, as was Brad Snyder, a freestyler who won gold in his 400-meter race in London, exactly a year after he lost his sight while serving in the Navy in Afghanistan. I knew them a little from the Paralympics and from the national team. Chasing them every day in practice was going to be exciting and was certain to make me faster.

Two others rounded out the para group in my freshman year: Alyssa, an S5 sprint freestyler and backstroker who would compete collegiate varsity for Loyola, like me, and Lizzi Smith, an S9 butterflier and club swimmer.

The para group was formidable, but what made the Loyola program even stronger was how we para swimmers were welcomed into the overall program. From the start, I was part of a competitive and supportive team and was expected to contribute as much as any able-bodied athlete.

I was up for the challenge, despite some ups and downs since London. Missing the World Championship squad in 2013 had been a blow, but I climbed back the next year, landing on the national team again after a solid performance at the Pan Pacific trials. Then at the Pan Pacific meet, a major international competition just two weeks before I left for Loyola, I swam poorly.

Ugh.

I realized at Pan Pacs that the training I was doing wasn't enough to make the big impact I hoped to make. That would change at Loyola.

Morning practices six days a week started at 6 a.m., and I made it a point to be early. This wasn't too difficult since I'm a morning person. Plus, I had extra motivation to not snooze because it's safer for me to get through the locker room and into the water without a ton of people around.

Weightlifting was part of our training regimen, too. I had never seriously lifted weights, and I quickly could see and feel the difference. I mostly lifted small weights with lots of repetitions, and my muscles became more defined, especially in my arms and shoulders. I felt stronger in the water, and I also saw other benefits. Like, I was able to get myself out of the pool without using a ladder, and I'd not always been able to do that.

We had afternoon practices every weekday. Meets were mostly on Saturdays.

Regular-season college meets are usually held in 25-yard pools and are dual meets, a format that encourages league and conference rivalries. Loyola's biggest rival was Baltimore neighbor Johns Hopkins University. When we swam against Hopkins, the meets were well-attended because both schools' in-town fans could come. It was always loud and fun, but Hopkins almost always destroyed us.

In my freshman year, I added to the chaos at the Hopkins meet with a for-the-record-books rookie mistake.

We were hosting the Blue Jays at the FAC, and since it was a home meet and our roster was so deep, Brian put together more relays than normal. What I didn't realize was that I was on one of them.

I heard my teammates frantically calling my name.

"McKenzie! McKenzie!"

Oh, no! Was I on a relay?! I hadn't even checked the list, so I ran over to the wall and scanned it for my name.

There I was—on the "D" relay, affectionately—and this time, appropriately called the "De-lay." I rushed to our lane, shoving my hair into my cap and adjusting my goggles along the way. I was the backstroker, so I'd be going first.

"It's a 400 right?" I asked an equally panicked teammate.

"Yeah, yeah, get in!"

Except, it wasn't a 400. It was the 200-yard medley relay, meaning I was to swim a 50 of backstroke, and when I touched the wall, the next person would dive in for 50 yards of breaststroke. Butterfly and freestyle would follow, but in this case, it hardly mattered—we're just glad everyone lived to finish the race.

Because when I got to the wall at the end of 50 yards of backstroke, I flip-turned and started the second half of what I thought should be 100 yards.

At the same time, our breaststroker dove in.

I'm pretty sure everyone in the whole place yelled "Oh, my God!" at the same time.

She narrowly missed landing on top of me.

We both could have been seriously hurt or worse, and it was absolutely my screw-up. I think I said, "I'm fine," a hundred times and, "I'm sorry," a hundred more.

Brian smarted off to me at the end of the meet. I deserved it.

"Yeah. Not my finest day," I remember saying. To myself, I was also thinking, *Thank goodness my mother wasn't in the stands!*

Brian has only been mad, like, vein-popping-out-of-neck mad at me, one other time.

It was, again, freshman year, and, for the record, he came in that day a little "off."

But he clearly was trying to shake his mood, so he announced a different sort of practice. We'd be doing sprint 50s off the starting blocks. It would be fun, he said, and there was some challenge or incentive, or something…I honestly can't remember, and that just goes to show why he got so angry.

I couldn't grasp the concept of the set. Neither could Alyssa, and the two of us were doing it all wrong.

"McKenzie! Alyssa!" he yelled.

"Are you even listening?! Are you even here?!"

"Just stop. Just don't even do it."

And we were told to get out. In front of the whole team! We were shocked, and so embarrassed, but we really had been being stupid, and that day was not the day to be stupid around Brian. I wouldn't let it happen again.

I trained mostly with Loyola's distance group, but sometimes I did the stroke or sprint workouts. A solid butterfly set is a good way to balance out all the distance yardage, and my stronger shoulders could handle butterfly better than ever before, thanks to the weightlifting.

Still, my scoliosis and hip inflexibility make it hard, so I'll never be a huge fan of the stroke.

Luckily, Brian didn't make me swim it in meets—until near the end of my senior year.

I hadn't done a 100 fly in a meet since I was 14 years old, and my performance that day was right up there with my rookie relay disaster. I absolutely died in the second half of the race. I'd rank it one step up from drowning.

That day, it was my turn to be mad at Brian.

Over the winter break, Loyola, like a lot of college teams, would take a training trip, usually to someplace warm, where we'd do crazy amounts of swimming and lie in the sun between two-a-day workouts. We'd use a long-course pool, so short course would feel easier upon our return. The timing of the trip coincided with the peak-intensity point of the college season, and afterward, workouts relaxed a bit, with an eye toward swimming fast at end-of-season championships.

Brian always tucks away a few workout gems for the winter training trip, including one called the "five-mile set." It's sort of an initiation, and everyone stresses over the suspense of not knowing when it's coming.

Each long-course mile is broken in different ways, starting with 15x100 meters, followed by 5x300, 3x500, 2x750, and ending with a straight 1500-meter swim for time. Sets like these are meditative to the point of hypnotic and are my favorite. I might've been the only one on the team ever looking forward to that set.

I was never the fastest swimmer for Loyola, which competes in the National Collegiate Athletic Association's top tier. My times, though, counted for Paralympic rankings as well as collegiate scoring, so I enjoyed the double dip. It was super fun to be entered in the mile, for example, and along the way, set Paralympic American records for my classification in the 200-, 500-, and 1000-yard freestyles before hitting the final wall at 1650 yards, or 66 lengths of the pool, with a new para record for the short-course mile, too.

The first time I did that, it was October of 2015. I was a sophomore, and the 2016 Rio de Janeiro Paralympic Games were on the horizon. It was also a triumphant comeback after the first major injury of my college years.

I broke my leg at work during the summer between my freshman and sophomore years. I was working in the laundry and equipment room of the FAC, my first real job besides coaching with my mom. It paid minimum wage and gave me free housing, both which I needed to stay in Baltimore and train with Brian over the break.

I worked by myself behind a tall counter, way in the back of the facility, checking out basketballs and other equipment to members, but since hardly anyone used the FAC during the summer, I mostly mindlessly cleaned and played card games on the computer.

I was Lysoling stuff the day I caught my foot in the strap of my own bag, which I'd left on the floor.

Please, tell me that didn't happen, I pleaded in my head. But I knew. I had heard it when I thudded to the ground—that telltale snap. My right femur was broken. Again.

I laid there for a moment and took stock of my situation. I knew I'd need to go to the hospital, but first, I needed to get off the floor. I reached for my desk chair, where my fashionable Longchamp bag's straps were tangled like tentacles in the wheels. I pulled myself into the seat.

Now, I could reach the phone, so I called for a manager.

I took deep breaths, closed my eyes, and tried to hold myself together. When I looked up, a man was in front of the counter, holding out his membership card. I exhaled, and noticed the manager, another student worker, had shown up. He had that deer-in-the-headlights look of someone who'd slept through employee first-aid training.

"Listen," I told him, slightly under my breath, so as not to draw attention. "My leg is broken. In a minute, you're going to call 911. It's important that you stay calm.

"But first, hand that man some ping pong paddles or whatever it is he wants, so he can skedaddle.

"I'm going to scoot on this chair, out of sight."

I could feel a muscle spasm coming on. *It's important that you stay calm*, I repeated to myself.

Manager-guy looked at me. The member, still waiting for whatever, looked at me.

"Uh. OK," my manager said. "But how do I scan his card?"

Did you skip employee orientation, too? I wanted to scream. But I didn't. Instead, I calmly taught him how to check out a basketball.

The ambulance arrival created way more of a spectacle than I had hoped for. Then, the paramedics grabbed me from my rollie chair to put me on the stretcher.

"No!" I yelled. "Don't touch me!"

They argued. "We need to stabilize," they said.

"I've had plenty of broken legs," I said. "I can tell you what I need to do. Just stand back."

Then, like a quarterback or a conductor, I started calling the shots. I told them what part of me to hold, which to move, what comes next, and together, we positioned my body onto the stretcher. At the last minute, someone again tried to grab my leg.

I lost it.

"No, no, no! You don't understand! I've dealt with this my whole life!" I yelled.

"I know how to do this. Don't touch me!"

What's the best way to panic your mother from 600 miles away?

Call her from the back of an ambulance.

"I'm on my way," she said.

What's the best way to alarm your coach?

Call him from the back of an ambulance.

"I'm on my way," he said.

It was terrible to call my mother with this news but having to call Brian was worse. On top of the physical agony I was in, I didn't want to disappoint him. An injury like this would set us back months, and just the day before, I had flown home from Glasgow, Scotland, with a relay medal from the World Championships. I was primed for a final push toward Rio, and we'd had every reason to think I'd be on the podium.

Except now I was calling Brian, hysterically crying, as sirens wailed.

It's important that I have someone at the hospital with me. While I have every respect for doctors, there's always the chance I'll get one who has never seen OI, or one who wants to experiment.

"Look at all these lines on your bones," they might say. "Let's do some screws!"

If I ever become unable to communicate, I need someone there to speak for me, to stop ambitious ER docs from taking me to surgery before my own specialists can weigh in. It's a 10-hour drive from Georgia to Baltimore, so my mom is not always going to be that person.

It's nice, too, to not be alone when I'm hurting.

Brian was good company in the emergency room. He's good in a crisis, amazingly even-keeled.

"How could I let this happen?" I cried to him. "What about Rio?"

"You're going to be fine," he assured me. "I'm not worried."

I lean on a couple of things to get me through ordeals like this.

Level-headedness is one. Humor is another.

Any level head will do, and it's not always mine. I am devastated when a goal gets pushed aside by my OI, and the disappointment is often worse than the physical pain. My mom and Brian, both utterly unflappable and eternally optimistic, are excellent foils. Their confidence in my ability to heal and overcome always fills-to-overflow any gaps created by self-doubt.

Hearing Brian say he wasn't worried about Rio as I lay on that ER gurney was exactly what I needed to keep me from spiraling into despair. Part of me felt guilty for asking Brian to come to the hospital that day. The rest of me will be forever grateful that he did.

Laughter comes with the passing of time. With the recovery of each trauma, an eventual layer of humor is left behind, and much like pamidronate built rings around my bones, my soul is strengthened for the next time I need to smile through adversity—or loan someone a basketball at an inopportune time.

In the most absurd of situations, people often say, "either laugh or cry," as if there's always a choice, and as if laughter is the preferred pick. In my experience, crying and laughing are intertwined, and I wouldn't trade one for the other, as both have made me who I am today.

Healing from the FAC break was complicated, and I required surgery and a bone marrow transplant. My mom stayed with me for a while, but school started two weeks after the surgery, and it was time to get back to normal. It was a hard start to my sophomore year, but I was grateful for the experience of navigating a major injury on my own, in my own life setting. It was the first time I had to do that, but it certainly wouldn't be the last.

I'd get another shot at injury self-sufficiency (*yay, me!*) soon enough.

In the middle of my sophomore year's second semester, after a successful college swim season that saw me break American para records in nearly every freestyle distance, I got pushed in a dorm stairwell one Saturday night during a fire drill.

Fire drills are routine in college residence halls, and I had a system for surviving them. I would walk to the stairwell and wait for the masses to pass. Then, I'd make my way down.

I followed my plan this time, too, but a few tardy students ran past after I thought everyone had gone. One brushed me, and it was enough to knock me off-balance. I caught myself, but I heard my shoulder pop.

On Monday morning, Brian noticed I was in pain at practice. I told him what had happened, and he left it up to me whether to swim. I did, but everything hurt. By the end of the week, I flew home to have X-rays and see my orthopedist.

"There's a small fracture back there," she said. "But swimming isn't going to make it worse.

"Just do what you can tolerate."

It was March of 2016. The trials for the Rio Paralympic Games were less than three months away, and I knew I could tolerate just about anything. So I flew back to Baltimore and got back to work.

My decision to keep swimming served a couple of purposes. First, it kept the forward momentum toward the Games. I had had enough interruptions to my training in the last quad, and I wanted things to be full steam ahead for Rio. Plus, I knew that swimming through pain would be a confidence booster. If I could swim strong with a broken shoulder, imagine how fast I'd be in June for Trials and in August for the Games.

How does an OI child visit Mickey Mouse or sit on Santa's lap? In her mother's arms, of course. My mother didn't let anyone hold me, out of fear that I'd accidentally break a bone, so the most memory-making events of childhood had to be carefully orchestrated to include me. I'm so glad everyone made the effort, even if it confused a few Santas and Mickeys.

Images show two Coan family photos. The first shows McKenzie Coan as an infant and her mother, Teresa, holding her while standing next to a person in a Mickey Mouse costume. Teresa has short, dark hair and is wearing short pants and a short-sleeved T-shirt. McKenzie's father, Marc, is kneeling to the left of Mickey. He is wearing short pants and a baseball cap. His right arm is wrapped around a small, light-haired boy who is McKenzie's brother Grant Coan. The second photo shows the Coan family with a man dressed as Santa Claus. Brothers Grant and Eli are sitting on Santa's lap. Marc, Teresa, and McKenzie are standing behind Santa. Teresa is holding McKenzie, who is preschool-aged. A Christmas tree is to the left of the group.

We grandchildren called my grandmother "Bye-Bye," a name bestowed by my older cousin because Bye-Bye watched him when my aunt would go out. Bye Bye came to help for a while after I was born, but I made her nervous, so seeing her holding me in this photo is special to me. My big smile shows it meant the world to me then, too.

Image shows a dark-haired woman with glasses holding a young, light-haired girl on her lap. The woman is wearing a long-sleeved shirt and a vest. The girl is McKenzie Coan as a toddler. She is wearing pants with a flower print. A young, light-haired boy stands to the woman's right. He is Grant Coan, McKenzie's brother. He is wearing a long-sleeved shirt with a dinosaur on it.

My childhood wasn't normal, by any measure, but that didn't keep me from the joy of a toy car or the silliness of swim hair. Living with brittle bones isn't easy, but I've always been able to snatch happiness and hold onto it. Moments like the ones in these photos helped me through the hard times.

Images show McKenzie Coan as a toddler and as a young girl. In the first photo, she is a toddler gripping the steering wheel of a toy car. She is wearing a striped dress with a bib around her neck. She is smiling. Her short, light-colored hair is pinned back on one side with a barrette. In the second photo, McKenzie is a young girl wearing a dark-colored bathing suit. Her lips are bent into a silly grin. Her hair looks dried out, and it is sticking up.

The town of Toccoa, Georgia, has a Halloween costume contest, and we entered every year. My mom made our costumes. The time Eli and I went as Frankenstein and Bride of Frankenstein, we finally won. We were both really excited because our competitive streak was already strong, even at such young ages.

Image is a photo of a light-skinned man with glasses, Marc Coan, and two children in Halloween costumes. The girl, McKenzie Coan, is wearing a dark-haired wig and has white makeup on her face to make her look pale. She is seated in her wheelchair and carrying dead flowers and a trick-or-treat bag. The boy, Eli Coan, is wearing gloves and a satin-like shirt. He also has white makeup on his face. He is carrying a trick-or-treat basket shaped like a monster.

Being a swimmer, I almost never had occasion or reason to dress up and feel girly, so I loved Valentine's Day dances with my dad. This was one of my favorite dresses, and I didn't let my dad see it before I was dressed to go. I'll never forget his getting teary-eyed when he saw me. My dad is a pretty good dancer and excellent company, so we had a great night!

Image shows two people, a girl, McKenzie Coan, and her dad, Marc Coan. McKenzie is wearing a long satin dress with a sheer shawl around her shoulders and arms. She is wearing dangly earrings, and her fingernails are painted. She is seated on a bench with Marc, and they are holding hands. Marc is wearing a sport coat, tie, and dress pants. He has a rose boutonniere pinned to his lapel.

I begged for a Yorkshire terrier for years before my parents relented and got me Ch-Ch-Chewie Chewbaca of Georgia, Chewie for short, for Christmas in 2008. He came into my life after a near-death post-operative nightmare, and he helped nurse me back to health.

Image shows a light-skinned girl with light-colored hair lying down and snuggling a small puppy with her right arm. The girl, McKenzie Coan, has painted fingernails and is smiling.

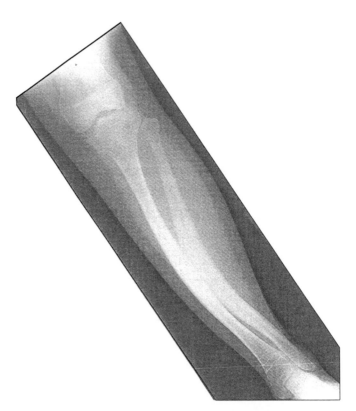

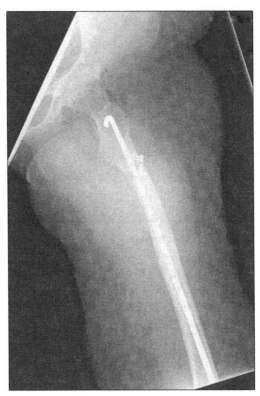

I've had hundreds of X-rays in my lifetime. These two images clearly show examples of my bowed legs and the hardware surgically inserted to help strengthen them.

Images are X-rays of McKenzie Coan's bones. One shows her lower left leg and the bowing of her tibia and fibula. The other is of her right femur, the bone in the upper part of the leg. A bright, straight line, which is a metal rod, and screws can be seen inside the middle of the leg bone.

My family works hard, but we always make time to vacation, too. We have enjoyed Maui together many times. I consider it our family's special place, that is where this family photo was taken. But nothing beats a trip with just my mom, and we loved visiting Paris in 2019. I had been there only once before—after the London 2012 Games—and I wanted to see the Eiffel Tower at night. It was beautiful.

Two photos show McKenzie with family members. In the first photo, Eli and Teresa Coan, both wearing sunglasses, are to the left of McKenzie, who is also wearing sunglasses. To McKenzie's right are Grant and Marc Coan. Grant has his arms resting on Teresa's and Marc's shoulders. Grant is wearing a baseball cap, and Marc is wearing a Hawaiian lei made of tiny flowers. Marc's shirt has the U.S. Paralympic Team logo on the right side. A bit of ocean can be seen behind the group. In the second photo, McKenzie and Teresa are taking a selfie in front of the Louvre in Paris, France. They are both wearing sunglasses and smiling.

I missed my junior prom for a swim meet, so I did it up big as a senior. I loved my pink, sparkly dress and my curled hair, a big change from my usual chlorine-soaked messy bun. My date, a friend since fourth grade, and I had the best time, even though my mom drove us to the dance in her minivan!

Image is a photo of McKenzie Coan and her prom date, Coleman Crooks, in 2014. They are standing in front of a door. Coleman, a light-skinned teenager with dark hair and short facial hair, is wearing a dark suit and a diagonally striped tie. He has his left arm behind McKenzie, who is wearing a gown with a shoulder strap decorated with rhinestones. The gathered bodice also has rhinestones. McKenzie's light hair is long and curly. She is wearing dangly earrings.

I swam the 50 freestyle, my first gold-medal swim in Rio, the day before this photo was taken in the Paralympic Village. I had hardly spoken to my family in a month—since leaving for training camp—so it was extra special to get to spend this day with them. My mom could tell by looking at me that I hadn't been eating enough, so she insisted on my having a McDonald's cheeseburger, even though it wasn't on my training diet. It was the tastiest thing I'd ever eaten.

Image shows the Coan family at a wooden table in the Paralympic Village in Rio. Mark and Grant Coan stand behind McKenzie, Teresa and Eli, who are seated. Marc is wearing a baseball cap. Eli is wearing a backwards baseball cap. All of them have lanyards around their necks. McKenzie's sunglasses are on top of her head, holding her long hair back out of her face. Teresa is wearing sunglasses. Multistory apartment-looking buildings are in the background.

My brothers, Grant and Eli, have been my biggest cheerleaders. Grant, shown here in the stands at the 2016 Rio Paralympics with a cardboard cutout of my head, is a gem of a big brother, always setting the example when it comes to work ethic and diligence. In the other picture, my younger brother and kindred spirit, Eli, and I are "twinning," wearing matching mascot hats in a Rio Paralympics gift shop.

Two images show McKenzie Coan's brothers, Grant and Eli Coan. Grant is shown seated in an aquatics center with a crowd of fans around him. He is looking at the camera and holding a large photo of McKenzie's head. He is light-skinned and has light-colored hair. He is wearing a collared, short-sleeved shirt. In the other photo, Eli Coan puts his left arm around his sister and leans toward her. He is wearing a T-shirt and shorts. He is holding his phone and wearing a lanyard around his neck. McKenzie is wearing a short-sleeved T-shirt and dark leggings. Sunglasses are hanging from her shirt collar. Both Eli and McKenzie are wearing hats that resemble the mascot of the Rio Paralympic Games.

I'll **always be** grateful to Glenda Orth and Pete Junkins, swimming officials in Georgia, who first recruited me for para swimming. It's a thrill to see each other at meets far from home, so we started a tradition of taking a photo on every pool deck we share. In the above photo with Glenda, we are in Texas at Nationals in 2011.

In the other picture, I am holding Pete's luggage tag with his name on it—the same one he used on his bag for the Atlanta Games—next to the warmup pool at the 2016 Paralympics in Rio de Janeiro. Pete had died earlier that year, so it was special to have a little bit of him there with me and my gold medals.

One image shows a light-skinned woman, Glenda Orth, seated next to a light-skinned girl, McKenzie Coan, in a wheelchair. The woman has her left arm behind the girl, and the girl is leaning toward the woman. They are smiling. The other image shows McKenzie as a young adult, standing in front of a swimming pool and holding a gold medal and a luggage identification tag. She is wearing a Team USA podium uniform and is also holding a stuffed toy. She is smiling.

I've had the good fortune to visit the White House twice as a member of Team USA, after both the London and Rio Paralympic Games. This selfie of me on the White House lawn was taken in 2012, just minutes before I was told to put away my phone. I felt lucky to have such a good seat to hear President Obama speak—I was in the front row. In the other photo, from 2016, I was stunned when President Obama knew my name and mentioned some of my accomplishments when I shook his hand.

Images depict two separate White House visits. The first shows a teenaged McKenzie Coan. She is taking a selfie, and behind her is the White House and a dais with the Presidential seal. People are seated on bleachers in the background. The second photo shows a room inside the White House. McKenzie Coan is seated in her wheelchair and looking up at President Obama. They are shaking hands. The president is wearing a dark suit, and McKenzie is wearing Team USA uniform apparel. Several other people are in the background of the photo, including First Lady Michelle Obama, then-Vice President Joe Biden, and a person in a dress military uniform. A photographer is seen on the far right of the photo, with a camera over his face.

I was so excited to share the news of my Adidas sponsorship with my college swim coach, Brian Loeffler. And I was so emotional on Senior Day, when I swam my last collegiate home meet. I am proud to have been a part of Loyola's varsity program, one of the few that actively seeks and involves para athletes. Because of my experience and Brian's influence, I plan to continue to raise awareness of collegiate opportunities for para swimmers and urge coaches and programs to create more spots for para athletes on their rosters.

Two images show McKenzie Coan and her college swim coach Brian Loeffler. In one image, both McKenzie and Brian are wearing Adidas-logoed T-shirts. They are smiling at the camera. Brian has dark hair and is wearing glasses. McKenzie has her long hair pulled back into a bun. In the other photo, Brian has his left arm behind McKenzie and her parents, Teresa and Marc Coan. McKenzie is holding a large photograph of herself swimming. Brian is wearing a short-sleeved, collared shirt and long pants. McKenzie is wearing a swim suit and a jacket. She is standing slightly in front and to the left of her mother, who is holding a flower. To Teresa's right is Marc, who is wearing long sleeves and long pants and a baseball cap. He is holding a flower bouquet.

Forgive me for freaking out and fan-girling when I was invited to Adidas World Headquarters in Germany, only to find myself spending a day with Australian swimming legend Ian Thorpe, the Thorpedo, who is also an Adidas-sponsored athlete. I love this photo, taken outside Adidas HQ, because it shows how professional athletes come in all shapes and sizes.

Image shows two people in front of a large, rectangular-shaped building on stilts. The tall, light-skinned man with dark hair is Ian Thorpe, an Australian Olympic swimmer, and the shorter, light-skinned woman with long, light hair is McKenzie Coan, an American Paralympic swimmer. Ian is wearing a light T-shirt and dark shorts. McKenzie is wearing black leggings and a short-sleeved T-shirt.

I loved traveling with my teammates, especially the para crew from Loyola, shown here in Puerto Rico in January 2020, just before the coronavirus pandemic shut down the world. It was such a gift to be part of the post-grad program, which allowed me to mentor the next generation of para swimming Loyola Greyhounds. In this photo, from left, are Stephen Machak, Keiichi Kimura, myself, and McClain Hermes.

Image shows four swimmers hanging on one lane rope made of plastic discs. They have their arms around each other's shoulders. They are all smiling. The man on the left, Stephen Machak, is wearing a dark swim cap and has dark goggles on his forehead. The man with dark hair to his right, Keiichi Kimura, has his eyes closed. The woman to Keiichi's right is McKenzie Coan. She is wearing a dark swim cap and mirrored goggles on her forehead. The woman to McKenzie's right is McClain Hermes. She is wearing a dark swim cap and dark goggles on her forehead. The pool deck is littered with fins, pull buoys, and water bottles. A short distance away, a group of swimmers is on the pool deck. People in the distance appear to be exercising on concrete stairs.

As much as I love my swimming friends, it's so nice to have non-swimming friends, too. My best college friend Elizabeth Hull and I met on the first day of our freshman year, and we became friends and study partners. We still hang out when I'm in Baltimore. Nick Adcock and I actually met through swimming, but he's a "swammer" now. He, too, lives in Baltimore, and is one of my most outgoing friends. He tries to make me jealous of his 30-minute "retirement" workouts. Nice try, Nick. I'm not there, yet.

Two photos depict McKenzie Coan as a young adult. In the first, she is to the left of her friend Elizabeth Hull. They are both wearing graduation caps and gowns. They are close together, shoulders touching, and smiling at the camera. In the second, McKenzie Coan is seated to the right of her friend Nick Adcock on the rim of an outdoor fountain. It appears to be nighttime. Both McKenzie and Nick have their arms crossed with their hands on their knees. Both of their bodies and heads are slightly tilted to the left. They are both smiling.

This photo of Colleen Young and me was taken at a meet in Germany in 2019. It's one of my favorites of the two of us, and that it was taken in Germany, where we first really became friends, makes it more special. I love Colleen for the way she makes me laugh and always has my back. She's also a badass breaststroker and a good roommate, even when she leaves her shoes in the middle of the floor.

Image shows two light-skinned women with long, light-colored hair. On the left is Colleen Young, a Paralympic swimmer. She is wearing a dark-colored swimming tech suit. She is seated and leaning toward McKenzie Coan. McKenzie is wearing a dark-colored swimming tech suit with a vertical stripe down the middle. An American flag hangs behind them.

This is the smile of a world record-setting world champion who didn't know she had mononucleosis or that she was swimming in her last meet before the 2020 Paralympics would be postponed over a global pandemic. Oh, ignorance is bliss! (Seriously, though, I was stoked to win the 100- and 400-meter freestyles at the World Para Swimming Championships in London in 2019, and collecting the 400 WR was the fulfillment of a dream. No wonder I'm beaming!)

Image shows McKenzie Coan, seated in her wheelchair and holding an American flag behind herself with both of her hands raised above her head. She is wearing a swimming tech suit with the Adidas logo on the right side. The dark-colored suit has a vertical stripe down the middle. McKenzie is also wearing a dark-colored swim cap and dark goggles positioned on her forehead.

I love public speaking, something I learned about myself way back in Girl Scouts when we had to give speeches. As a Paralympic champion, I've been invited to share my story with groups as varied as bigwigs at Adidas Headquarters and second-graders in Baltimore public schools. One of my favorite speaking opportunities was with Olympian Kara Lynn Joyce's annual LEAD Summit. LEAD stands for Leadership, Empowerment and Athletic Development, and the summit attracts teenage girls from around the world to learn about confidence, mental health, perseverance, and more. I was honored to be the summit's keynote speaker in 2019.

Two images show McKenzie Coan. In the first, she is seated at a restaurant to the left of Olympian Kara Lynn Joyce. Both women are light-skinned with light-colored, long hair. They are smiling and have plates of food in front of them. Kara Lynn is wearing a baseball cap. McKenzie has dark sunglasses hanging from the neck of her shirt. She is also wearing a denim jacket. In the second photo, McKenzie is standing beneath large balloons shaped like the letters L, E, A, and D. She is gesturing toward the balloons and wearing a LEAD Summit tank top. Two square, framed pieces of art are hung on the wall behind the balloons.

My smile here says it all: Not even a broken pelvis or a 10-hour drive was going to keep me from attending my friend Jessica Long's wedding in 2019. I'm so happy my mom was able to drive me from Atlanta to Baltimore, the last leg of a 4,000-mile round trip, to be there in time. I have admired Jessica since she gave an inspirational talk at my first para swim meet when I was 8 years old. She is one of my swimming heroes and a dear friend.

Image is a photo of two young, light-haired, light-skinned women, Jessica Long and McKenzie Coan. Jessica is wearing a wedding dress with a plunging neckline and spaghetti straps. She is leaning toward McKenzie, with her left arm behind McKenzie. McKenzie is wearing a dress with a high neckline, made out of a crepe-like fabric. She is wearing a necklace. Both women are smiling. A wedding guest is eating in the background.

When the COVID-19 pandemic shut down the pool at Loyola University, I returned to my parents' house in Georgia. Pools there were closed, too, so we bought a pop-up tank for the garage. Since I was attached to a tether and waves kept hitting the walls and splashing back at me, it was like swimming on a treadmill in a washing machine.

Image shows a woman swimming in a small pool inside of a home's garage. The woman is McKenzie Coan. She is wearing a swim suit, a swim cap, and dark goggles. She has a tether attached to a belt around her waist. The garage door is open, and it is daytime outside. Interlocking pipes give the pool its shape. The walls and floor of the pool are made of a heavy tarp material.

In September of 2020, my mom dropped me off at the Olympic and Paralympic Training Center in Colorado Springs, where I could live in a sheltered "bubble" during the coronavirus pandemic. On-campus athletes were required to quarantine upon arrival, and then agree to not leave, so virus transmission could be curtailed. It was such a relief to have this safe environment at such an uncertain time. Plus, I was excited to join a group of athletes who all shared my experience of a delayed Paralympic Games.

Image is a selfie of two women outside a white building. Both are wearing masks that cover their noses and mouths. The woman on the left is Teresa Coan, mother of McKenzie Coan, who is shown on the right. Teresa has long, dark hair, and it looks wind-blown. McKenzie is holding her identification card for the Olympic and Paralympic Training Center.

CHAPTER SEVEN

RIO

Before the Trials for the 2016 Paralympics, I was due for a classification appointment.

On the international para-swim circuit, classification appointments typically happen every two years, or whenever a change in status or disability warrants one. My appointment in 2016 was routine, but I was expecting a reclassification. Since my last appointment, there was a new rule, called the "minus one" rule, which subtracts one sport class if the swimmer is of short stature, on top of having other impairments.

I qualified as being short, so even if nothing else were different with my OI, I expected to come out of this appointment, at most, an S7.

The entire process unnerved me, knowing I'd be pulled and poked, twisted and tested. I prayed I wouldn't be hurt in the process.

I flew to Berlin, Germany, for the appointment, which included a physical assessment, where it was determined I was under the "minus one" threshold; a technical water test where I was asked to perform certain skills; and an observation in competition, to see to what degree my disabilities impaired me when I was racing.

Unsurprisingly, I left Germany an S7 (S6 for breaststroke). This was good. I would be once again competing against swimmers of similar impairment. But also once again, the change was bittersweet. No one likes being told they are more disabled today than they were yesterday.

Additionally, my appearance among the S7 ranks was not universally welcomed. My name on the list shuffled the world rankings, and that ruffled some of my competition.

I was quickly the subject of rumors and bullying, and I refuse to give either more fuel or satisfaction, then, now, or in the future. My S7 assessment was legitimate and fair. It happened within the rules and parameters of World Para Swimming. I challenge anyone who might be similarly affected by a newcomer to do what I do when the situation is reversed:

Swim faster.

I qualified for the 2016 Rio Paralympic Games in five events, the 50-, 100-, and 400-meter freestyles, 50-meter butterfly, and 100-meter backstroke. I also would have a chance at a relay.

It was, perhaps, most surprising to find myself in the 50 freestyle, the usual domain of quick-twitching sprinters with powerful starts and lung capacity to spare. Few 400 freestylers also train for the 50, but Brian had studied the field, and he knew I could make an impact in the short stuff, too, if I were interested.

"There's no reason that you can't be a great 50 freestyler," he had told me, sometime in my sophomore year.

So we started mixing it up—maybe doing a sprint workout in the morning, and keeping with my usual distance yardage in the afternoon. Taking a lesson from my training ahead of London, I insisted on a 50 free, for time, at the end of every practice. I sometimes had to drag myself onto the blocks, but I came to know I could be fast when I was already tired, and the repetition of every day, all-out sprinting bred confidence.

Still, it took a mind shift to embrace the sprints. Growing up, Eli had been the "fast one," and I was the steady distance swimmer. There was satisfaction in the longer races, and I couldn't help sometimes feeling short-changed by the 50 and 100. They were over way too soon!

My presence in the backstroke and fly wasn't too unusual, but I wasn't considered to be a medal contender in either event.

I was limited in my backstroke training because when I'm on my back, my ribcage smashes my lungs, so I don't get sufficient oxygen. To practice backstroke, I swim mostly freestyle, and then I switch every third or fourth lap to backstroke. This is enough to be pretty good at the stroke but not a force. That being the case, we considered the 100 back to be my warm-up event in Rio. It was first in my program, and it would serve to shake out the jitters.

Even though my body limited me to only short bursts of butterfly, swimming the 50 at Rio would work to keep me occupied and loose between my freestyles. Butterfly would be third in my order of events, after the backstroke and 50 free, and before the 400.

The relay was the day after the 400, and the 100 free would be my last event of the Games.

While London had been a wide-eyed whirlwind, Rio would be all business. I finally had a full Paralympic program, and with it came renewed and amplified pressure. In the two months between Trials and leaving for Rio, it seemed like everyone was asking if I was excited, and if I was going to win, and how many gold medals I was going to bring home.

I was asking myself the same questions, and sometimes it was just too much. So I retreated into my bubble, stayed off the internet, and tuned people out. That way, I could focus on the answers: Yes. Yes. And lots.

Two weeks before the Games, Team USA headed to training camp in Houston. I was looking forward to being a veteran this time, not a scared newbie. I was ready to be a team leader and to put in the work.

All was going according to plan, until it wasn't.

Early in camp, we were practicing backstroke starts and breakouts with a quick set of eight 25s. On the third one, I arched too much, and I felt a snap, low in the back, on the left side of my ribcage. I quickly popped up. "Oh, my goodness!" I gasped, but not too loudly. I got myself out of the pool and over to the athletic trainers. When they touched me, I nearly jumped off the table in startled pain.

I had a decision to make, and fast. I asked myself, *How big of a deal is this? Do I really want to know?*

Nope, and here's why: I knew I could quickly lose control of the situation, and with it, I'd watch my goals and dreams go down the drain. I didn't want to be treated with kid gloves or have anyone think I can't manage my disorder. I didn't want my competition to find strength in my weakness.

I knew I could swim through pain. So I swallowed hard and quit wincing.

"I'm fine," I told the trainers.

We went through team processing soon after we landed in Rio. It was again a fabulous overabundance of gifts and glory. We were showered with jackets and workout clothes, suits, caps, and goggles. We also were sized for our Paralympic ring, which is like a school-class ring. You get to pick ways to personalize it, and it comes in the mail a few weeks after the Games.

I held the order form and looked at the choices. There was a check box next to "Gold Medalist" (and silver and bronze). It would take a special kind of confidence to mark the "gold medal" box.

Why do they make you order this ahead of time? I agonized. *Is this really so much more efficient?*

I really, really wanted to check that box.

So I did, but I also wrote a note: "If I win gold, could you put this on there? If I don't, don't worry about it."

Many swimmers, in the weeks before a big competition, cut back on their training to recover and refine details instead of continuing to pile on the laps. I'm not one of those swimmers. I don't rest easily, and I crave consistency, so I don't taper my workouts much, even for the Paralympic Games.

This was both good and bad going into Rio. Mentally, I wanted and needed status quo, but soldiering on through the rib pain was physically tough. I remember a particularly rough day once we got to Rio, a few days before the Games started, when we were practicing relay exchanges. My reaction time was a little off, so I was getting yelled at, which I understood because no one knew the whole story.

After the workout, I grabbed my swim bag and found a quiet spot beside the warmup pool. I laid face down on a mat and just sobbed. After a bit, I got my phone out of my bag and called my mom.

"Mom, how could this have happened?" I cried. "I'm 20 years old, and I feel so helpless! I've worked so hard to be here. How can this be happening?"

I was terrified someone would see me crying, but I couldn't stop.

"Everyone is expecting so much!" I told my mom. "I will do everything to do my very best, but what if it isn't enough?"

"McKenzie," she told me, "do not underestimate yourself. You are strong. And it will be enough."

The day after my big cry, I was feeling better. I had gotten it all out in sobs and snot on that mat at the side of the pool. Plus, my mom had recommended some breathing exercises that were both therapeutic and calming.

All along, the pain had been the worst when I was diving. Once I was in the water, adrenaline and muscle memory took over. My body knew what to do, and it would get its first chance on Day 1 in the 100 backstroke.

I'd always been a middle-of-the-pack backstroker, so my goal was to swim my fastest and make it to finals. I wanted to test out the pool, go through the call room, and get used to the excitement and hype while swimming a relatively low-key event for me. The rib ordeal had thrown me off, so I was also anxious to compete and put it behind me.

That morning, I arrived for the preliminary session so early that I was the first person in the pool. I felt peace and wonder wash over me as I started my warmup. I floated and looked up at the ceiling, scanned the stands and marveled at how quiet it was. I knew it was only a matter of minutes before a cacophony of a hundred languages, whistles, music, splashes, and horns would break the tranquility.

I soaked in the stillness and reflected for a second on all the hard work I had put in to get there. I knew I had done everything I possibly could, good days and bad, and I felt confidence take over any doubts.

After warmup, I saw my parents in the bleachers. Seating wrapped around the Olympic Aquatics Stadium, and the lowest row was close enough to the pool deck that we could have a quick conversation. They were worried about my ribs.

"How do you feel?" they asked.

"I'm fine. I'm ready," I assured them.

"You got this," my mom told me, and she was right.

I put on my racing suit, warmed up again, and went to the call room.

I'm not going to lie. That backstroke start hurt. But the rest was exactly what I wanted: a best time, a trip to finals that night, and an eventual fifth-place finish. The boost that came with that swim would carry me through the entire meet.

This would be my Games, my moment.

The 50 free came on the third day of competition. I felt loose in warmup, and my rib wasn't bothering me. *Today is going to be a good day*, I remember thinking.

I was in the second heat of prelims, and I tried not to worry about anyone or anything else. I kept my headphones on and my eyes down in the call room, but I couldn't help listening when they announced the times from the first heat.

Huh. OK, I thought. *They were really moving.*

I took a deep breath, or at least as deep as I could. It was time to go to our blocks. I wheeled out to get in position, and I adjusted my cap. I pushed my goggles against my eyes to create more suction and fiddled with the goggle straps.

Instantly, surprise and panic set in. My goggle straps should have been underneath a second swim cap. I had forgotten my top cap!

In big meets, it's common to wear two swim caps. The first one covers your hair. Then you put on your goggles and wear a second swim cap to prevent the straps from moving and your goggles from falling off, especially when you hit the water on your start. The top cap gives peace of mind. It's also sleek and makes you look like a superhero.

Well, nothing I can do now, I told myself, and I got on the block for a sprint to the other side.

I swam my hardest. My goggles stayed on, but they wiggled just enough to fill with water by the end of the 50 meters. When I looked at the scoreboard, I could barely make out the words "Paralympic Record."

Wow! I wonder who did that? I thought.

I looked again. There was a number 1 next to my name and my time, 32.57 seconds.

I was ecstatic. A Paralympic record!

I'm seeded first for finals! I thought to myself, nearly bursting with excitement.

And then, *Oh, crap! I'm seeded first for finals!*

I got to briefly see my parents and Brian in the stands before leaving the venue. I told them how nervous I was, how excited, and how I had no idea how to pull that off a second time. Also, did they see how tall some of those Chinese swimmers were? How was I supposed to compete against that?

"Let them chase you," Brian told me, "but don't let them catch you. You're number one. Keep your head down, get out in front, and stay there."

We took a group picture, and then it was time for me to rest. It was a 40-minute ride between the pool and my bed at the Village, plenty of time to think and be thankful, and I found myself overcome with joy.

My fears about the tall Chinese swimmers were not unfounded. Two of them would be in the finals with me that night.

In the call room, Rihanna was turned up in my headphones, and I kept to myself, wanting to stare at the wall, focus, and visualize my race. But I felt someone watching me, and I turned to see a very tall Chinese competitor hovering.

I moved to a new spot. She followed. I moved again. There she was! Too close.

Oh, no. We are not doing this! I thought to myself. *Back up. I can take you out, and I can take you down,* I told her in my head, and I gave her angry looks. I'd never felt such intentional intimidation in a call room before, and I was reeling. I was, like, DONE. I was not about to let her psych me out.

But she kept lurking, and I just got madder.

I forgot my top cap again for the final. And my start was weak. I don't remember much else, but when I look at the video, my face shows how pissed I was when I rolled out, and how I pulled away from the field at about the 35-meter mark.

Then I see how anger gave way to ugly crying at the finish. I was stunned at my place, first, and my time, :32.42, another Paralympic record. I had won gold!

Afterward, I was able to lock watery eyes on my mom and dad and Eli in the stands (Grant hadn't yet arrived in Rio). Then I was whisked to warm down, and I shared a huge group hug with my teammates.

Before long, I was putting on my podium gear. Everyone gets a special podium uniform at team processing. But not everyone gets to wear it on the podium at the Games. I hadn't worn mine in London, so putting it on in Rio for a gold medal ceremony felt like a long-awaited privilege.

The medal was heavy, and I forgot to step back from the front of the podium. And even though I tried, I couldn't stop my tears through the flag raising and the national anthem. My mind flashed back through a lifetime of swimming memories, and I was so grateful.

After the ceremony, I found my family and Brian. I couldn't wait to hug them. What I didn't realize, though, was that you can't just walk around with a hunk of gold hanging from your neck. I was swarmed by fans in the stands. It was sweet and unexpected, and I appreciated the attention, but it honestly wasn't safe. Eli went into bodyguard mode.

"Back up! Give her some space!" he directed.

Then, to me he said, "I knew you could do it!

"I just never thought it would be in the 50 free!"

"I guess I'm full of surprises," I said. "And I'm not done, yet."

I had a day off before the 50 butterfly, which was supposed to be another low-stakes swim. The down time, plus already having one medal under my belt, left me feeling a lot more relaxed. I was happy with my 50 fly prelim swim, which put me sixth going into finals.

I almost always swim faster at night. The prelims get me warmed up, and then it's all-out for finals. But not in the 50 fly at Rio. I finished sixth in the final, which was OK and about what I expected, but I added time from my morning prelim, which was a huge disappointment. I tried to not let it show. Cortney Jordan got silver, and I was happy for my Loyola swim partner, so I smacked a smile on my face and turned my focus and energy to the 400 freestyle, which would be swum in two days.

The next day, though, we got some unexpected news. Two swimmers had scratched the 400 free, so the preliminary heats were being scrapped. The top eight swimmers in the 400 were automatically advancing to finals.

"Only one swim?" I asked the staff person who told me. I was concerned. There'd be no psyching up, no getting a feel for my competition.

"Only one. And we think you can win it.

"What do you want to do?"

They were asking how I wanted to spend the morning. Typically, we were required to be at every session, even if we weren't swimming.

But this was different. The dropped prelim could throw me off my game, so I was shown some grace. I would be allowed to stay in the dorm and rest.

That morning in my room, all by myself, was bliss. It had been nearly a month since leaving for training camp and being around people all day, every day. I used the quiet time to think through the race coming up that evening.

I sat on the floor, set a five-minute timer, and closed my eyes. Then I visualized my 400 free—the start, every arm stroke, every lap, every turn, touching the wall in my imagination as the timer buzzed. When it was time to leave for finals, I was in the perfect headspace.

At warmup, I was again the first one in the pool, a special start to what I knew was going to be an epic night. I felt great, and I even got to quickly talk to Brian—him hanging over the railing from the stands.

"Go do your thing," he told me.

"Yeah, this is going to be a fun one," I told him.

In the call room, I couldn't stop smiling.

I was in lane four for the 400, the top seed. I took the lead of the race in the first 25 meters, and I never looked back.

I swam a very even race, finding my up-tempo pace quickly and not slowing down. I averaged about 38 seconds per 50 meters, and no one ever challenged me for the front position. When I touched the wall first, in a time of 5:05.77, I had put a 13-second cushion between me and the rest of the field.

As I hung on the wall, exhausted and elated, it was as if I had the whole pool to myself, and in a way, for those 13 seconds, time stood still. I got to have my own moment, and I'll always be grateful for that.

Gold medals are not won in a silo. Even in swimming, considered by most to be an individual sport, victory is a team effort. Coaches, family, teammates, strength coaches, nutritionists, mental performance specialists, and many others all play a part, and without them, there is no glory. So when the *Star-Spangled Banner* played during the 400-meter medal ceremony that night, I pulled up Cortney Jordan, my training partner and the silver medalist, to share the top spot with me.

Why would I share the spotlight with a competitor?

The answer is simple. It felt like the right thing to do.

I had two events left. Both were 100-meter freestyles.

The day after the 400, I was the leadoff leg of the 34-point 4x100-meter freestyle relay. In para swimming, relay teams are designated by a point system. In the 34-point relay, the sum of every swimmer's classification cannot exceed 34.

I was the only S7 on the relay, which was also made up of Lizzie Smith, one of my Loyola teammates who was an S9; Jessica Long, an S8; and Michelle Konkoly, an S9. It's unusual for a 34-point relay to be made up of only 33 points. If I hadn't been swimming so well, I would not have been picked. Typically, another S8 would have filled out this particular team, since an S8 should be faster.

So performance pressure was high, plus my rib was hurting. I was nervous, to say the least.

Do not mess this up, I told myself after learning I'd be on the relay. *Do not let anyone down. It's time to deliver.*

I got some needed support from my teammates.

"You've got this," Michelle said. "You've been killing it.

"Let's do this."

The four of us suited up in our podium jackets and made a bit of a scene walking unified and stoic to the call room. We were pumped, and we looked mean and ready to go. But when we got to the call room, the guy at the check-in desk was, like, "What are you doing here?"

"Huh?"

"The meet is running, like, an hour behind schedule. Come back later."

Good grief.

When it was finally time to report, we tried re-creating our badass arrival, but we pretty much just laughed all the way there.

Being the first relay swimmer, I had a regular, flat start. I finished my leg in sixth place, which meant there was some ground to make up, but considering everyone who touched ahead of me was in a less-disabled class, sixth place was right on par. My split was 1 minute, 9.41 seconds, which was a great time for me.

I've done my job, I thought. *Let's see what the rest of us can do.*

My teammates rocked the rest of that relay. We got second, finishing fewer than four seconds behind the Australians, who set a world record. To take the podium with my three friends for the silver medal was a huge honor and a lot of fun. It was nice to have some levity to offset what was to come: the 100 free, my last event of the 2016 Paralympic Games.

After my 400 freestyle, a reporter asked me, "Do you think you're going to win the Triple?"

What does that even mean? I wondered to myself.

"I'm sorry," I said out loud. "What is the Triple?"

He explained that the Triple was winning every freestyle event in the S7 class in a single Games. I already had won the 50 and the 400. Winning gold in the 100-meter freestyle would give me the Triple.

"Do you know how rare that is?" he asked.

"Well, I guess I do, now."

In fact, no one had ever done it, at least under the current classification system. No pressure there, right?

Throwing down that 1:09 on my relay split gave me confidence, and when it came time for the 100 free prelim, I channeled all that energy. I went 1:09.74 and dominated my heat. I would be the top seed for finals.

And then I got tired.

It was Day 9 of the Games. I had only 100 meters left to swim, but I was suddenly and absolutely beaten down. I tried to give myself a pep talk.

You're awesome. You can do this. You've done sets of 100 repeats off the blocks, 40 times over again. There's no reason you can't do this twice today.

But I was freaking exhausted, seriously crashing. The Triple talk had worn me down.

There is no replay, I told myself. *You don't want to be the girl who almost did it, but just missed it. Just go do this, and afterward, you get a break. You don't even need to warm down, if you don't want to.*

My internal cheerleader wasn't getting anywhere. I felt "meh" in warmup for finals. So I got my tech suit on and found a quiet spot to listen to music and try to turn things around.

My eyes were closed when one of the staff approached me and lifted one side of my headphones.

"We're one gold behind Great Britain," they whispered.

"Excuse me?" I asked.

"We're one gold behind in the medal count. You need to go out and win this."

Are you kidding me? I thought. I honestly was shocked to get this pressure, 10 minutes before I was to report to the call room.

I looked at the staff person, hoping for at least a smile of encouragement, but all I saw was stone-faced seriousness. Nothing else was said, and the person walked away.

To say I got fired up is an understatement. Were all my accomplishments only tally marks?

Screw that! I thought. *I have done my job here. I have done everything! I am more than a medal count! This is my last race of these Games, and I'm not going to let the medal count ruin it for me. No matter what happens, I will enjoy this last swim.*

When I got behind my block, all I could think was, *One and done. Go have fun.*

I swam that 100 free on autopilot. All my training kicked in, and I didn't have to think at all. The last 15 meters hurt more than any race before or since, but the pain faded as soon as I touched the wall and saw the number one beside my name.

Cortney got silver, again, and the Chinese swimmer who'd seemingly tried to intimidate me in the call room got third. I never wanted to leave the podium that night.

When the ceremony was over, though, I had my most special experience of the Games. I went to the stands to find my family (this time, hiding my medal in my jacket). I was talking to people and taking pictures. At the back of the crowd waiting was a little girl in a pink wheelchair. I took out my medal and let her hold it. She put it around her neck. In halting English, she told me that she and her mother had come from somewhere far away in Brazil, just to see me swim.

"And I want to be just like you," she said.

I was awed. I thought back to the London Games and its theme of "inspire a generation." Right there in front of me, half a world away in Rio de Janeiro, was tangible and living proof of that inspiration. She might have looked up to me, but that small girl would, in fact, inspire me forever going forward and would always be a reminder to me—if I ever needed it—that the Paralympics matter much more than just the medals.

CHAPTER EIGHT

COMING HOME AGAIN

Re-entry to real life was rough.

I caught food poisoning in the airport before leaving Rio. Ick.

I got an X-ray, and, indeed, my rib was broken. Duh.

I returned to school, my junior year, a month behind in my classes. Yikes.

And more than any post-London letdown I experienced, I felt an underlying sadness, which made everyday hiccups, like a healing bone or playing catchup in class, harder. On top of things, everyone expected me to be happy. I'd had so much success, after all. What was there to be depressed about?

Success was at the root of it, though. Now that I had three gold medals, I had a target on my back. I had become the one to beat, to knock off the Paralympic podium in Tokyo in four years. Being chased instead of doing the chasing would require a big mental adjustment.

I felt like I was failing everywhere, too, especially in school, where I'd always been an "A" student. Before leaving for Rio, I'd been in touch with my professors and academic advisors, and whatever work I could do ahead of time, they mostly provided me. I worried about my classmates' perception of that. Would they think I'd gotten undue special treatment?

Even with the accommodations and having snatched moments in Rio between events to study, when I got back to campus, I was drowning in assignments, projects, and tests.

I found myself irritated at basically everything, even my friends. I resented their laid-back lives. For the past several months, since making the Rio roster, I'd been under so much scrutiny, not just with a demanding schedule, but also with sleep, diet, and socializing. When I got back to Loyola, I couldn't relate to anyone.

I was pretty detached from reality. I wasn't myself. I needed to regain control of what I could, and that started with school. I took time off from swimming to concentrate on academics, and I visited all my professors' office hours to glean as much extra time and knowledge as I could. In one class, though, I was hopelessly behind, and the instructor was unwilling to help. It killed me to drop that class. I felt like I was giving up. But to dig out of the hole I was in, I had to lighten the load.

Several weeks later, mid-terms provided a reset for everyone, and I felt on equal footing again. I could finally breathe.

More is being done these days to provide mental health support for Olympic and Paralympic athletes, and I'm here to say it is needed, necessary, and still not enough. We've always had sports psychologists to help get us to the medal stand. What happens after we win needs just as much investment, for the sake of decency and compassion, but also self-interest. Because for anyone to return to the podium, the scaffolding needs to be there.

Post-Rio was perhaps the biggest rut I've experienced that seeped from one part of my life—swimming—into others, like school and my social life. But there have been other trying times and triggers.

One of the most obvious and enduring emotional hurdles comes from discrimination over my disability, and while it's been hard for me, my mother has often had a more difficult time. It's hard to watch someone you love struggle.

Early memories of discrimination are mostly hers, like when I was denied a spot at school in the violin vs. fiddle confusion. Once, too, when I was 8, my mom remembers kids staring at me in a store. They wouldn't leave me alone, so I stood up from my wheelchair and exclaimed, "It's a miracle!" They ran fast.

Adults weren't much better. A stranger once asked what was wrong with me, wondering if I'd been in a car accident. I told her no, I just hadn't eaten my fruits and vegetables.

A little sass goes a long way, but as I've gotten older, I've fought discrimination by helping to educate at the source.

After falling and breaking my pelvis in January 2017, in the second semester of my junior year, I was asked to give a presentation to Loyola's ADA Compliance Committee about how Loyola could be more accessible to students with disabilities. The ADA is the Americans with Disabilities Act, a civil rights law that protects against discrimination.

My presentation led to an on-the-spot job offer from the Student Development Office, the same department I'd blown off in my freshman year, and which helps all students to get the most out of what Loyola has to offer, including services for disabled students. One of my biggest assignments was to help create a map that highlights all the accessible elevators on campus, as well as the paths and routes that are safest for people who use wheelchairs. I also identified places on campus where signage was lacking, making accessible building entrances harder to find, so more and new signs could be posted.

Additionally, I steered a partnership with the career services department to educate disabled students about accessible employment laws and to provide networking opportunities.

I continued to work in Student Development past graduation, even after the coronavirus pandemic forced my departure from Baltimore in 2020. (I worked remotely.) It is my sincere hope that my efforts there both made life easier for disabled students and helped to create a world where life is easier in the first place.

When I broke my pelvis in 2017, the doctor said I should be dead.

Yeah, that'll do a number on your mental health.

I'd fallen in a campus lecture hall, having tripped on a carpet when I was walking with a heavy backpack instead of using my wheelchair. I was so embarrassed. I knew better, and I hated having to call campus police and 911.

Can you cut the sirens? They seem a little unnecessary, I remember thinking.

My mom came to help me. We lived in a hotel for a couple of weeks, where we had more privacy and space than in the dorms. We found creative ways to use the hotel furnishings as lifts and stretchers, and I shoved a washcloth in my mouth to muffle my screams when I needed to move. We kept the lights low, I'd lay in bed, and my mom would sit, quietly watching me slowly heal.

I needed to see a specialist, but it would be impossible to travel home. We made an appointment with someone closer, setting in motion what has become one of my worst memories.

When we got to the appointment, the doctor entered the room, making no introductions.

"I've seen all your films," the doctor said, "and I'm appalled. I don't know how you're alive. Have you seen your lungs?"

Respiratory problems are the leading cause of death for people with OI. I know people who have died from pneumonia and other respiratory diseases. *Did they think I didn't take these things seriously?*

"Do you know how bad your lungs are?" the doctor asked.

Where was this hostility coming from?

"Ummmm," I said. "I've been dealing with this my whole life. My parents and doctors have always told me the truth. No one sugarcoats anything for me, so, yes, I know the state of my lungs, and I'm always careful," I said.

The barrage continued.

"Your back X-rays are horrendous. Your scoliosis is out of control. I have no idea why your back isn't rodded. Do you walk?"

"Yes, part of the time," I answered, cautiously.

"That's shocking to me!"

If we'd been boxing, I would have been the fighter backed into and slumping on the corner ropes. I summoned all my energy to defend myself.

"You know, I'm in pretty decent shape. I swim seven days a week. I just got back from the Paralympics in Rio, so I'm pretty sure I'm doing OK."

"Swimming?" the doctor questioned. "I don't know how you're still doing that. You can forget about that because you're going to move into a rehab facility for the next two years. And if you don't, you're probably going to die."

It took everything for me to hold it together, and as much as I didn't want this one doctor visit to affect me, in the weeks after, I started second-guessing myself. My brain was filled with crazy thoughts: *Am I in trouble? Am I physically not OK? Am I going to die?* My mental performance consultant and my mom helped me put things in perspective.

"When in your lifetime," my mom asked me one day, "have you ever let anyone tell you what you are capable of?"

Never.

Yet I'd never needed the reminder more. Looking back, the worst thing about this experience wasn't the assault or even the distress afterward. It was passing the parents and children with OI in the waiting room on my way out of the doctor's office.

"Run for your lives!" I wanted to tell them. "Don't let this doctor scare you! Just because someone has fancy degrees saying they are an expert in your disability, it doesn't mean they are an expert in you. Your OI life can be full and happy and strong. You can study and learn and travel and work and win gold medals. You will have friends and find love."

I have known romantic love, and I have known heartbreak. I prefer the former, though I have little time for either.

Swimming makes things complicated. It's my full-time job, and I lift weights, watch my sleep, and I eat carefully. This commitment means I'm not often the life of the party, and anyone I might be in a relationship with has to accept that. With the Tokyo Games, law school, and hopefully future Games still in play for me, I'm not compromising the habits that have made me successful.

OI makes things even more complicated. I don't want to burden somebody who maybe doesn't know what he is getting into. I'm nervy about being touched, and I'm aware that I look different. When I start to click with a guy, I'm likely to hold back, thinking, *Wait. If I'm sharing my life, it becomes his life, too. He didn't sign up for this.*

This is an easy hang-up for disabled people. Believing someone has an interest in you and that they accept your inconveniences takes super-human self-confidence. And when a relationship doesn't work out, the down ramp is ready. At least, this was the case for me once. His new girlfriend being able-bodied made things even worse.

It's not like I didn't already know hurt and pain, but that just flat-out sucked.

I know there will be other guys, and when I meet someone who I can trust, who won't freak out when I break a bone, who is a calming presence and a friend, he'll be the one. He won't have to validate for me that I'm "good enough," either. I've worked through and answered that question for myself, and I know that I am. It took a while to come to that conclusion, though.

It's not easy to be the only one rolling into class or around the pool deck. It's not easy to scroll social media and see pictures of pretty, normal girls doing pretty-normal teenage things when there's nothing normal about how you live, and you don't always feel pretty. It's not easy to see your body both deteriorate with disability and bulk up in ways not always considered feminine or attractive.

With maturity, though, I've come to be happy in my own skin. I'm proud of my scars and my chair, my rods and my muscular arms. They all make me stronger, and my beauty is in my strength. I'm confident now in saying, "This is what I look like, and this is how I get around. If you like me, great. Let's get to know each other. If you don't, it's not going to keep me up at night. I gotta get up for swim practice, anyway."

When it comes to love, I prefer to remember a sweet guy from the Rio Games, who kept flirting, even when I tried to ignore him.

He was on the U.S. soccer team, and he seemed to always be in the cafeteria when I was, usually a table away, but often looking in my direction. His gaze was actually kind of irritating, even though he was super cute with jet black hair and a nice smile.

"I think he likes you," a friend said.

"No," I replied. "Just no."

After a couple of days, he sat at the table with me and my friends, butting into the conversation. Again, I was annoyed, so I tuned him out.

"Why are you so quiet?" he asked me.

"I'm focusing," I told him.

"You focus, like, 24/7?" he asked.

"Yes. Yes, I do."

The morning of my 400 free, when I stayed behind in Team USA House to rest, I saw him in the common sitting room. I had gotten a snack and stopped to watch some of the televised swimming heats. Not a minute later, Soccer Boy was there.

Not this guy again, I thought to myself.

"What are they swimming?" he asked. And he tried to make small talk, but it was painfully awkward. Plus, I was on the middle couch cushion, and there was nowhere for him to sit without creating personal space issues. I stayed put, and he kept standing there. Still annoyed, I could finally read his vibe, and I had other things to worry about. I went back to my room.

Eventually, he won me over with a chocolate churro.

He held out the pastry for me to take one day when we were in the cafeteria.

"Thanks, but I can't eat that," I told him.

"Come on, you can have one bite."

"I really can't. I'm still competing."

"It's not gonna kill you. Just have a bite," he said.

I ate the whole thing, and it was delicious.

We started talking, and I liked him.

Don't get distracted, I told myself. *Only one more event.*

He asked me about my schedule. "What do you have left?"

"I have the 100 free tomorrow."

"I'll be watching."

OMG! Like I need any more pressure! So annoying! I thought, and I immediately shoved him out of my mind.

But the day after the 100 free, we exchanged numbers. I saw him at the Closing Ceremony, too.

"What are you doing later?" he asked when I bumped into him.

"Oh, nothing much. We're not allowed to go out."

Swimming was always the strictest of the sports at the Games. While other teams were checking out Rio nightlife, we were not supposed to leave Team USA House.

He was disappointed.

"It's OK," I told him. "We'll find something fun to do. Or maybe even just go to sleep. We're all exhausted."

He texted me later.

"You still up?"

I was.

"Come to the second floor. I have a surprise for you."

When the elevator door opened, he was standing there, holding a beanbag chair he'd snatched from his room.

"Let's go," he said.

"Where are we going?"

"To the roof. It's still 'in the building,' right?"

"Yeah, maybe, but, um, I don't really know you."

"I'm not going to throw you off the roof," he said. "I promise."

We rode the elevator up, and then we climbed a staircase to the roof. When we opened the door, two para swimming coaches were already there.

Crap.

"Oh, hey, McKenzie," they said. And then they turned around and pretended they hadn't seen us.

Soccer Boy put the beanbag down, put his arm around me, and we took in the city lights.

In December of 2017, nearly a year after cracking my pelvis and receiving the grimmest outlook imaginable for my future, I won the 100- and 400-meter freestyles at the para swimming World Championships in Mexico City.

That next spring, I finished my final swim season at Loyola. I cried behind the block before my last race.

"Oh, God. You're crying," Brian deadpanned, and I laughed, but I also choked back a sob, and the tears filled my goggles over the whole 66 laps. I broke the American record for the women's S7 mile that day, as well as for every competitive distance along the way.

I had about 20 minutes over the course of that swim to reflect and rejoice, and at the end, I hugged Brian and my parents, knowing a big part of my swimming career had just come to an end.

College swimming was over, and I would graduate near the top of my class in a few short weeks with a political science degree.

I wasn't in a rehab facility. I wasn't dead. I was happy, whole, strong, and proud, and it was time to think about what would come next.

CHAPTER NINE

EYES TOWARD TOKYO

The end of my senior year marked the midway point between Rio and what we thought at the time would be the 2020 Paralympic Games in Tokyo. Promotions were already happening in Japan, and I had caught the attention of a video crew that worked for a network there called WowWow.

They wanted to include me in a series of documentaries about Paralympians, so their producers came to Baltimore from Tokyo and followed me around. They recorded me at the pool, around campus, making peanut butter toast, and while taking my last final exam. They followed me to graduation, even trying to interview the girl in line to receive her diploma ahead of me.

"How do you know McKenzie?" they asked her, like it was something special to be standing next to me.

"Um, I just met her, like, five minutes ago. It's, like, just alphabetical order here," she said, rightfully confused.

Thankfully, that didn't make the documentary's final cut.

The end of school was an exhausting whirlwind. I had some of my hardest classes in my last semester, I was training with Tokyo in mind, and I moved into my first apartment just days before graduation. (Eli might never forgive me for leaving that IKEA furniture for him to assemble.)

It was in the lobby of my new apartment building that my life took its next important turn.

After Rio, many people had encouraged me to become a professional athlete, to capitalize on my gold medals and get sponsorship money.

"You never know if you'll get another chance," was the refrain.

I was never really tempted, though. I wanted to have the full student-athlete experience, and that required me to not earn money from swimming until my final college season was over. I also was confident in my having another shot. Tokyo was my goal, and nothing was going to keep me from it. The sponsorships would be there, even if it meant waiting for them.

Once my NCAA career was done, though, there was no reason to not pursue professional opportunities. So just days after graduation, I sent an email to a handful of sports agents.

My mom and I had studied each agent's portfolio. Do they already represent para athletes? Would they want to?

One agent replied that they weren't looking for new clients. We never heard from another. Then, another set up a call, just a few days after graduation. There was only one hitch: the cell reception was terrible in my new apartment!

So I sat in the public common area of my building to take the most important call of my life. The agent, Cejih Yung, asked me about my goals, both in swimming and in life. He wanted to know how he could help me achieve them.

I talked to him about the Paralympics, world records, about advocacy, and how I planned to go to law school. I told him I want people to look at me and know they can do anything they put their minds to, and that different abilities should be celebrated, not pitied. I told him how my competitiveness first came out when I was selling Girl Scout cookies, and that my favorite cookie was Samoas, hands down.

Saying all that, out loud, to a stranger, was scary. Plus, who knows how many of my new neighbors were listening and now knew my entire life story? I swallowed hard, summoned some courage, and kept going. I told him I wanted a swimsuit sponsor. I wanted to do public speaking. I wanted to write a book.

And then Cejih said, "Let's make it happen."

I'm pretty sure the whole building could hear my enthusiastic agreement.

Less than a month after turning pro, I set my first world record at a meet in Berlin, Germany, in the women's S7 800-meter freestyle. By the end of 2018, I added the world record in the 1500.

I had continued to train with Brian at Loyola as part of his club program of post-grad and other para athletes. I felt lucky to have this as an option, and I enjoyed both the successes and some new training partners who had sought Brian's expertise ahead of the Tokyo Games.

I formed a special friendship with Keiichi Kimura, a butterflier from Japan. He'd been featured by WowWow, too, so we had something in common from the get-go.

Keiichi is blind, so he doesn't drive. I started picking him up for practice in the morning. And even though he uses a white cane to get around, sometimes my eyes are more reliable, so when we walk together, he'll hold my arm.

When it's icy or the ground is uneven, it's nice for me, too, to have him there, so I don't fall.

He says I'm quiet before practice, but on the drive home, I won't stop talking. Our car-ride conversations have helped Keiichi to learn

English, he says, so I'm glad my coffee and workout endorphins eventually kick in!

In the fall of 2018, both Keiichi and I swam in a meet in Japan, so I got to see Tokyo through the eyes of a local. I fell in love—with Tokyo, that is—but photos of Keiichi and me together that were posted on social media created a buzz and speculation that we were a couple. We laugh, but it's also a good reminder to me about how social media always tells a story, whether it's true or not, and to be careful. When I started talking to sponsors, they wanted to know what type of things I post and follow online. I'll never forget being asked, "Who are you on the internet?"

I was glad I'd never posted anything I wouldn't happily show my parents, which turned out to be a good guide. Yes, you need the medals and records, but the personal side matters, too, when you want to sign a sponsorship deal.

I felt like Cinderella when the Adidas racing suit samples fit.

It's hard for me to find a good tech suit. I'm short, and my upper body is out of proportion to the rest of me. Sizing me is part measuring, part magic. I tried the Adidas suits first at home, and then at practice. They felt tight in all the right places, and I was fast in them, too. I sent an email to my Adidas contact: "They're perfect."

He responded right away, even though it was the middle of the night in Germany: "You have no idea how happy I am to hear this. We'll send the contract over in the morning."

Cejih and I had talked about what would be a fair amount of compensation. I'd turned down an offer with another brand because I didn't think it represented either what I'd done or my potential.

When I opened the Adidas contract, I couldn't stop the happy tears from flowing. Their offer exceeded my dreams, and it gave me hope. It proved that they really looked at me like I was worth something, and that meant the world.

I soon visited both Adidas North America headquarters in Oregon and Adidas world headquarters in Germany. To get an idea of how that went, think team processing on steroids. Plus, in Germany, I met one of my swimming heroes, Ian Thorpe, who is also an Adidas athlete. In Portland, I learned that singer Pharrell Williams had sat just a week earlier in the same chair I was using. I was star-struck.

That summer, Colleen came to live with me, so we could train together for the 2019 World Championships. It was a roommate situation made for a TV sitcom, and I loved having her there, even if her air mattress was always in the way.

In September at World Championships in London, I won the 400- and 100-meter freestyles, narrowly missing the world record in the 100.

But the tidal wave I was riding toward Tokyo came crashing down not a month later.

In October 2019, I broke my pelvis again, this time in the gym at Loyola. I was walking with a 15-pound weight, and I fell. Fifteen pounds!

My lift coach, Deanna, came running.

"Can you get up?" she asked.

"I really can't. I've done something, and it's starting to hurt," I told her.

Cue the chaos. Trainers started pacing and planning.

"OK," they said, "we're going to pick you up and carry you to the car."

"No, no one's touching me. Please, get my wheelchair," I said.

They ran to get my wheelchair and came back with nothing.

Oh, no! I'd walked that day!

"Here's what we're going to do," I told them. "A wheelchair is just a chair with wheels. Someone get an office chair."

Carefully and deliberately, I got onto that office swivel chair, and they rolled me outside and down the sidewalk to my car, which Deanna had moved and parked, ready to take me to the hospital.

Once we got there, we sat. I waited with Deanna, and later Brian, for 12 hours, long enough for me to see more than one fight break out and to notice a very jaundiced man maybe die next to me. (I don't know. He looked almost dead, and I dozed off. When I woke up, he was gone.) My mom even had enough time to drive to Atlanta, board a plane, land in Baltimore, rent a car, and drive to the hospital before I was seen.

After getting some initial treatment, my mom and I decided it would be best for me to see my doctor at home, but first, I was scheduled to speak at the Gulf Swimming annual meeting in Houston. I was able to sit up, so we drove.

After two days in Houston, we were off to Atlanta. My doctor confirmed the broken pelvis, but there wasn't much to do about it except to let it heal. Jessica Long was getting married the next day in Baltimore, and I didn't want to miss it, so we drove.

In all, my mom logged a 4,000-mile loop for me, over only a few days. Despite my discomfort, it wasn't all bad. We devoured drive-through Chick-fil-A and watched movies in hotel rooms. We speedily bought a beautiful coral-colored dress at a TJ Maxx just 30 minutes away from the wedding venue, and we laughed about how crazy this all was while trying to get me ready in the dressing room.

I missed my mom when she went home, so in a way, what happened next had a small upside. Only two weeks after she left, she came back. I needed her. What started as a sore throat soon after the wedding turned into an abscess on my right tonsil, and it was obstructing my airway. If it were to burst, it could cause pneumonia, so this was an especially complicated predicament for me. Antibiotics didn't help, so it had to be aspirated with a needle. I was worried the numbing agent wouldn't be compliant with the drug testing regulations that I'm required to follow as an athlete, so the doctors drained it without painkillers. The stupid thing was stubborn, too. It took them more than a few tries.

I'm not going to lie. That ranks way up there on my list of painful medical procedures.

Then, blood work I'd had as part of the tonsil treatment revealed mononucleosis, which I'd had possibly for weeks—at least since the World Championship meet. Just think, without mono, maybe that 100 free world record already would be mine.

One more crushingly sad thing happened in 2019. My beloved dog Chewie, who had carried me through some of my toughest and darkest days, died at the age of 11.

Surely, better days were to come in 2020.

CHAPTER TEN

PANDEMIC POSTPONEMENT

Wrong.

The first couple of months of 2020 passed typically-enough, for me: two major earthquakes while on a training trip to Puerto Rico in January and a bout of flu in February that required an ER trip.

Knowing what we know now, that flu is suspicious.

The first cases in the United States of COVID-19, the illness caused by a novel coronavirus that led to a global pandemic, were reported in February. By March, much of the country was in various stages of lockdown to stop the spread of the disease that was killing people all over the world.

Loyola's campus, including the aquatics center and my office in Student Development, was shuttered. I was both distraught and optimistic. The decision to close the pool seemed an overreach of protection, so I was confident the closure would be temporary.

Knowing what we know now, my reaction was naïve.

I followed the advice of health experts and stayed mostly at home. COVID-19 attacks the lungs and causes coughing, fever, chills, and a multitude of other symptoms. The more I learned about it, the more scared I became. Some people with COVID-19 said it was like breathing glass shards or like bees were stinging their lungs. My lungs, vulnerable from OI and asthma already, could not take a severe COVID infection.

It was lonely and boring in my apartment, and I stressed about how swimmers in other cities, states, and countries might still be able to train, since restrictions varied from place to place. In desperation and out of a sense of duty for being on the national team, I rigged a "swimming machine" out of a coffee table, resistance cords, and some swimming hand paddles. I laid on the table and mimicked freestyle with my arms, the paddles attached to the stretchy cords, which were tied to a towel rack on the bathroom door.

That got old quick.

By the end of March, it was clear there was no end in sight, either to the local lockdowns or the spread of the virus. One night, I sat on the floor of my apartment and thought, *I feel like something really bad is happening. This thing is not going away.*

I felt suffocated by helplessness. I had to find a way to cope, and that meant taking control of my own situation. I couldn't just sit and wait, anymore. So I decided to leave Baltimore and go back to Georgia. Things were different in the South. Rebellious. Life would be a little looser there, and with the Tokyo Games still on schedule, I needed to find some water.

I didn't know at the time that that water would end up being a 7-foot by 10-foot soft-sided tank in my parents' garage.

Or that within a week of arriving in Georgia, the Tokyo Paralympic Games would be postponed until August 2021.

I never sleep in. I really don't. But pandemic living upset all sorts of routines, so one night soon after getting to my parents' house, I was, like, *I'm not going to set an alarm.*

So I was asleep when Brian texted at 8:30 a.m., with a link to a news story announcing the postponement of the Games. What a world to wake up to, so strange and disheartening. But I understood.

The Japanese could not play host to thousands of athletes and spectators, risking everyone's health and safety, when it looked like COVID-19 would continue to rage into the summertime.

This is so much bigger than sports, I thought. *People's lives come first.*

Of course, I was sad, too. I had spent the past three years living for my chance at Tokyo. I had put swimming ahead of all else— willingly, but with a goal in mind.

Now what?

I gave myself a couple of days, and then I looked for the positive. "This gives us a little bit of a breather," I told Brian. "And it gives me another year to get better."

I had brought my coffee table swim machine from Baltimore to Georgia, and we set it up in my childhood bedroom, a place both familiar and foreign, my having outgrown its girlish decor.

"I know a lot of people have it way worse," I told my mom one day. "But I miss Baltimore. It feels like I've gone backwards, like I ran away from my life."

The pools where I had hoped to swim in Georgia were, in fact, closed, so I worked out on the coffee table twice a day, doing intervals and counting arm rotations. In between "swim" workouts, I lifted weights in our home gym, and I studied for the LSAT, the law school entrance exam. I'd taken it once prior, but now that I had extra time, I figured, why not try to improve my score?

As the outlook for normalcy dimmed, though, I knew I needed another plan. So I ordered from the internet a pop-up pool for the garage. The pool had a frame made of snap-together steel poles, and the bottom and sides were made of the same material as river rafts, so it was sturdy and tough. When filled, it would be 4 feet deep, and I could swim in it attached to a harness or tether to stay in place, so it was like swimming on a treadmill. It would take up exactly the amount of space as my dad's car, which would be relegated to the driveway.

He wasn't thrilled with the idea.

He wasn't wrong that it was a little crazy. When the kit arrived, not all the pieces were there, and once we had all the parts, it took my mom and me two tries to set it up.

"Oh, my God!" my dad exclaimed when he saw us, standing there, holding the tether rod and not having anywhere to attach it.

"This is completely wrong!"

"Um, we kinda already know that," we told him, and we took the whole thing apart to start over.

For the record, my dad helped us the second time. He's a good sport. But I'm pretty sure both my parents were ready to murder me.

I think they should have been mad at Eli, instead, though, who conveniently waited until the pool was in place before he came home from the University of North Carolina. Could his timing have been payback for when he put together all my apartment furniture? I'm pretty sure it was.

He was also suspiciously absent the day we flooded the garage while trying to change the pool's filter and a valve was stuck open. What was supposed to be a two-minute maintenance project ended with me jumping in fully clothed, not stopping the surge, my mother trying, also not succeeding, and then my mom running, sopping wet to a neighbor's house and asking a muscled worker there to come help. He took one look, and like flipping a light switch, closed the valve, but not before water several inches deep covered the garage floor.

"Huh," we said, taking stock. "That was interesting."

After a minute, my mom snapped to it.

"We better get this cleaned up before your dad comes home!"

Workouts in the tank were challenging, both mentally and physically. Typically, I would warm up without the tether, swimming just one or two strokes before touching the wall and turning around. I'd do this for a dizzying 20 minutes. After that, I'd maybe do 20 repetitions of alternating one minute of swimming and 10 seconds of rest. To mix things up, I'd then count arm strokes, first 50 arms, then 40, 30, and 20, all with 10 seconds rest, and I'd repeat the pattern 10 times.

Sometimes, I swam a little bit of butterfly, but the splash back was too much to do it for long. Sometimes, I used a kick board, but my fins make my body line longer, so I kept slapping the side of the pool. Sometimes, I'd alternate hard swimming and easy, long strokes—anything to make for a little variety.

Eli, who was on the swim team at UNC, blasted music through his workouts. I swam in silence. We swam singles at first, but we bumped it up to twice a day by August. We took turns in the pool, and we both lifted and studied in between.

My workouts were an hour to 90 minutes long, and at first, the longest I could keep going at a stretch was for seven or eight minutes. That improved to 10 minutes, and I consider this a true accomplishment. The waves in the small pool made it feel like swimming in the open ocean. Or a washing machine.

I was still working out in my parents' garage in September 2020, past when the Tokyo Games were originally to have taken place.

By then, though, more was known about how COVID-19 was transmitted and how to mitigate its risks. Pools and other public venues were open in some places, closed in others, and more options were coming available every day.

I was grateful to have had my family and the comforts of home for the past six months, but it was time to make another move.

I decided to go to the Olympic and Paralympic Training Center in Colorado Springs.

I could live in the dorms, eat in the dining hall, and train with Resident Coach Nathan Manley. The campus was observing a strict "bubble," meaning everyone who came to stay there would first quarantine for two weeks and then agree to not leave, so the chances of COVID spreading among the OPTC residents were significantly lessened. Considering my being at high risk for severe infection, the OPTC bubble provided a measure of safety I could get nowhere else.

Plus, Colleen was there already, so I knew I'd have at least a little bit of a social life.

I'd lived at the OPTC before, for a couple of months ahead of World Championships in 2017, so I knew some of what to expect: a 50-meter pool, weight rooms, top-notch sports medicine specialists, mental performance consultants, and a full-service cafeteria where, pre-COVID, we could go at all hours and get whatever we wanted to eat, including the best soft-serve ice cream on the planet.

The OPTC, in pre-pandemic times, could house more than 500 athletes at a time in dorm-style accommodations. Some of the dorms are nicer than others—the oldest are converted from when the complex was an Air Force base and are still called the "barracks."

Resident athletes get their own rooms, but bathrooms are shared and down the hall.

In a COVID world, however, the campus felt like a ghost town (and the ice cream machine was unplugged). While I quarantined to make sure I wasn't harboring the virus, food was delivered to my room in the barracks, left on a tray outside my door. Weights and other exercise equipment were also delivered, so I could work out in my room.

I was bored staring at the walls. I'd sometimes stick my head out into the hall and listen for anyone else in the building. It was almost always quiet. I tried to use the time wisely, and between workouts, I applied to law schools. Some days stretched so long, though, that I would take a shower in the middle of the day, just to break up the monotony.

I was excited to finally join the handful of other swimmers at the pool—*a real pool!*—once my quarantine was over. It had been half a year since I'd left my apartment and my independence, even longer since swimming in a legitimate facility. I felt such freedom in finally diving in. I exhaled the breath I felt I'd been holding since Baltimore, and I watched my bubbles float up, escaping with tiny pops on the surface.

CHAPTER 11

UNPRECEDENTED TIMES

This story is ending on a cliffhanger.

When it comes to the Tokyo Paralympic Games, rumors, opinion, and speculation are more common than concrete news. I tune out the talk.

Vaccines are becoming available, and at the same time, the virus has mutated. Will vaccination outpace the virus? Will the world be safe enough to let the Games begin? It's too soon to know.

We also don't know when the pandemic will end. And even when it does, we don't know in what ways the world will resemble what we remember. We are living in what has become a COVID-era cliché—"unprecedented times."

That the pandemic will leave us forever changed is the only sure thing.

Some changes will be common to us all—I'm hoping the heightened standards of cleanliness stick, for one. Other changes will be personal. In fact, a year into living in a COVID world, I've noticed an evolution in myself.

First and most importantly, I've learned I cannot be in control of everything, no matter how driven, focused, scheduled, ambitious, or competitive I am. Sometimes, I'll be forced to yield, and sometimes I need to yield voluntarily. Either way, I need to not be afraid of letting go.

Before, I was a catastrophic thinker, worried that the worst would happen if things didn't go according to plan. Now, I question what "the worst" even is, and when letting go of expectations, I know I can still function.

My mental performance consultant helped me to realize this. When I arrived at the OPTC, while glad to be there, I was pretty freaked out, too. I'd be living differently, eating differently, and training under a different coach. How could this be a good thing?

"What if this completely derails me?" I asked my consultant.

"What if it does?" she asked back. "Why don't you answer that for me?"

"Well, I'm not going to do well in Tokyo, if that's the case."

She pressed me for more. "What if Tokyo doesn't happen?" she asked. "You're giving up everything you know right now, yet you're still training. What if there is no Games?"

Thinking about that possibility takes the air out of me, but I knew the answer.

"I wouldn't be doing anything differently."

When I first got to Colorado Springs in fall of 2020, only a few athletes were at the OPTC. We commiserated over our dream's loss of imminency. Our training plans and the rest of our real lives would, at best, be pushed back an entire year. At worst, they could be on hold longer.

Over time, the athlete roster at the OPTC grew. As of spring 2021, I am part of a core group of para swimmers that has formed a tight bond.

I like the workouts with Nathan. His style is more finessed compared to Brian's bulk. I feel well-prepared after years of yardage to now be fine-tuning. Practices are still plenty hard, and I appreciate Nathan's eye for detail and his input into how to tweak aspects of my stroke based on my strengths.

My teammates, too, have buoyed me. While I miss my Loyola crowd, being around people at the OPTC who have this one shared experience—the delay of Games—has made the postponement easier to accept.

Between practices, hanging out in the OPTC lounges and lying across single mattresses in our dorm rooms, my friends and I plan for our futures. We talk a lot about Tokyo, but we chat just as much about weddings, jobs, school, and family. Amid all the uncertainty of this pandemic world, what's for sure is that we all have lives beyond the Games, and we're looking forward to them.

For me, that means law school. I got in!

Pre-pandemic, I wouldn't have entertained these conversations. I would have kept my thoughts, feelings, and words focused on swimming. Most everything else was a distraction.

After these last few months, though, of not being in control of where swimming will take me, sharing my fears about that with others who understand, and exploring all options, I find myself more open, both to people and ideas. I breathe easier. And I like it.

The pandemic forced me to let go of the rigidness that shaped my life, and I know now a relief I didn't realize I needed.

Swimming is still number one, but the pandemic has revealed other important things, too. And I'm happier for them.

Official word is that the Tokyo Games will proceed as announced and planned in 2021.

I'm operating under that assumption and training to the best of my ability. I'm swimming fast, too, so that's exciting. I fully expect to be on top of the Paralympic podium this summer.

It's hard to ignore the whispers, though. I won't be surprised by last-minute changes.

So what if Tokyo doesn't happen?

Catastrophic thinkers thrive on "what if" questions. We imagine misfortune and chaos. I'm learning to reframe those thoughts.

So what if Tokyo doesn't happen?

I'll give myself a couple of days to grieve. And then, like when a broken bone sidelines me, I'll tuck away the sadness and disappointment—not to dismiss either, but to make room for resilience. It will be time to figure out what's next. I could let the uncertainty around the Games consume my thoughts. And, yes, it's always playing in the background. But I love a good cliffhanger, so I let the suspense motivate me, and I keep swimming.

CHAPTER TWELVE

PARTING THOUGHTS

The London Paralympic Games' slogan, "Inspire a Generation," stays with me, all these years later. I expect this sentiment and the Games themselves will shape me for a lifetime.

I was born just a few weeks before the 1996 Games that were hosted in my home state of Georgia—I can't help but wonder what part destiny played? I intend to bring things full circle by continuing to compete until 2028, when the Paralympics is back in the United States, in Los Angeles.

The Paralympic movement is growing, and I always want to be part of its progress. To see disabled athletes recognized in the U.S. for being equal to our Olympic counterparts, and to know the impact that recognition will have for the larger disabled community, well, I don't want to miss out on that!

Plus, I can think of no better storybook ending than to end my swimming career on home turf in front of a hometown crowd.

I think a lot about the little Brazilian girl who came to watch me swim in Rio.

Did she join a swim team? Does she love the water? Does she dream big and work hard? Does she break through boundaries? Does she prove people wrong?

I wish this for her and all little girls.

I think a lot about the kids in hospitals, too. The trauma of childhood hospitalization never really leaves you, so that's why I will always visit sick children through Kenzie Kares, an organization I created when I was a teenager.

It is my mission to soothe and bring cheer to children in hospitals in the ways my family did for me—empathetic conversations, art projects, bedside manicures, books, and even by sometimes rolling a snow cone machine through the halls. If someone wants to hold my gold medals, I'm glad to play show-and-tell, too.

But these visits are not about me, despite their bringing me so much joy and personal healing. They are about support, understanding, distraction, and diversion, all to make things a little easier for pediatric patients, especially the ones with OI.

May those children find strength, possess courage, and overcome fear. May they defy expectations and shine with hope.

AFTERWORD

by Kara Ayers, PhD
2004 Paralympian

I met McKenzie Coan at a 2010 swim meet in Cincinnati, Ohio, after her mom connected us in learning that we were both para swimmers with osteogenesis imperfecta (OI). She'd learned that I lived in the area and asked if we'd like to connect. I'd completed my swimming career a few years prior after representing Team USA in the 2004 Paralympic Games in Athens, Greece. In some ways, I'd never felt further from swimming. It was Mother's Day weekend and my first as a mother-to-be. I rolled into the swimming arena, excited to see old friends and aware that I was about as out-of-swim-shape as you can get at around seven months pregnant on my barely four-foot frame. McKenzie's mom and brother immediately welcomed me to her cheering section, and their love for McKenzie and passion for our shared sport was immediately apparent.

Throughout my swimming career, I was almost always the only swimmer with my disability, OI. When you are "the only" for so long, it's surreal to see someone who shares so many things in common. The graceful beauty of McKenzie's stroke immediately struck me. If you haven't SEEN her swim, you must. It's almost indescribable, but I'll try. Her glide is beautiful. Her kick is a nonstop complement to her speed, but OI only offers so much in the leg strength category. McKenzie optimizes all of it. Even more impressive, she's a smart swimmer. As I've watched her progression in both sprint and distance events, you can see the pay-off of her deep study of swimming. She is humble and authentic as she looks to the leader board in shock, but for many of us, it's no surprise that she's become the most prolific athlete with OI in history.

While I'm not surprised, I'm no less in awe of McKenzie's journey to excellence. I derive much of my admiration from what others have not seen and don't know. Most people think the most painful or most difficult aspects of OI start with a broken bone and end with its healing. McKenzie and I, and so many others in the OI community, know that the lesser known aspects of OI can be the most challenging. As McKenzie shares with such bravery, OI can instigate the perfect storm for anxiety. Despite best laid plans, fractures emerge from the shadows to completely turn our lives upside down. In those moments of realizing what's happened... again, we also realize—with lightning speed—who we might disappoint and what we will now miss because of our injury. It is, of course, entirely out of our control—no matter what precautions we take—but hearts and minds don't always reach this consensus.

It is not uncommon for children and adults with OI to experience anxiety. I am now a researcher who studies the psychological experience of living with OI. The traumas of childhood fractures and hospitalizations can revisit us unexpectedly. Before her medals, McKenzie was already giving back to hospitalized children through her Kenzie Kares initiative, and she provides an invaluable gift to children and adults with OI in sharing her story as a Paralympian. McKenzie has shared, "My scars, my chair, my rods, and my muscular arms.... They all make me stronger, and my beauty is my strength." This message is often the first time a young person with OI has considered that they, too, can be beautiful and strong WITH their disability not despite it.

In learning about OI, some people come to the mistaken conclusion that our particular disability must only be a source of pain. There's so much more to OI than a list of symptoms or a running tally of fractures and surgeries. The OI community is rich in resilience and pride. We've learned powerful lessons about what matters most, and even amid crushing disappointments, we often find gratitude for what remains. When traditional methods don't work for us, like dancing on two feet or squeezing into an Uber-tight tech swimsuit without twisting and pulling, we innovate. We are problem-solvers and persisters. We've learned to rise up again and again because we have to. And because we know our comeback will be that much sweeter. Imagine doing all of this with the weight of a team, a country's hopes, and your own dreams on your shoulders.

The Japanese word "Kintsugi" means "to repair with gold." It is an art of joining pieces of broken pottery with golden lacquer. The pot is seen as more beautiful for having been broken. McKenzie's gold medals are just the beginning of the ways she will and has made us proud. Her golden gilded moments have emboldened her to live without regrets. Her mindset, drive, and smile (everywhere but the call room) are contagious. She brings so many incredible assets to the sport of swimming, Team USA, the Paralympic movement, and our OI and disability communities. It has been a true gift to share in a bit of her story. May we all make waves like McKenzie and no matter what, keep swimming.

ACKNOWLEDGMENTS

I cannot begin to express my gratitude to all who made *Breaking Free* possible.

First and foremost, thank you to my family—especially my parents and brothers. You taught me from the very start that I was never limited and that I should always listen to my heart and chase my dreams. I would not be where I am today without all of your love, support, and selfless sacrifices. Breaking Free is for you.

To my wonderful parents, I know it couldn't have been easy, but your strength in raising me just like my brothers, and never allowing me to feel any different, gave me the confidence and courage that I could pursue anything my heart desired. You taught me that just because I was differently-abled, it didn't mean I was limited. Like any normal little girl, I could dream of being a princess or a fashion designer, even letting me play dress up in a hospital gown, decorating it with my BeDazzler. You always found a way to ensure I was included in every family activity and event—even the chores I so annoyingly completed, sometimes in a full-body cast from a wagon. On top of the day-to-day hurdles we've faced, there have been difficult times that we've weathered together. Distinctively, in 2008, after one of my worst surgeries, I recall being in the ICU, waking up in bits of consciousness, but always seeing both of you in the room before going out again. Never once have you left my side, and I will never forget that. Early on in my para-swimming career, when I told you that I wanted to be a gold medalist, your first words were, "Okay, how can we help get you there?" It didn't matter the crazy goal or dream I was setting out to accomplish—you've always supported me. Looking back, I now realize how huge that is to have your parents' full support, and I will never forget all that you have done and given to get me here. Every time I step on the blocks, I take you with me and remember that I would not be here without you. You are the reason I survived, and I owe you everything. I love you both more than I could ever say.

To Grant and Eli, I know it probably wasn't ideal or easy to grow up with a sibling that required a lot of attention and care in dealing with a disease like osteogenesis imperfecta. I'm sure there were moments you wished things were different or easier, and I completely understand that. Despite that, you both have been by my side through the good and bad. Whether at a swim meet cheering or by my bedside after an injury, reassuring me that it would be okay—thank you for always having my back. I can't imagine how difficult it was at times, but please know I will never forget your sacrifices and support.

Growing up swimming as a swimming family was something I will cherish forever. The water gave us something to share and love, finding our unique talents and places within the sport. I watched in awe of Grant's flawless rhythm as a middle-distance swimmer, and as a distance swimmer, I tried hard to grasp the concept of sprinting from observing Eli's swift sprinting skills. Though the 3 of us all had different talents, one thing is for sure, no Coan could ever swim good breaststroke, and I'm happy to share that inability with my brothers.

Outside of the water, I've learned all kinds of things from you.

Grant, you taught me about work ethic in and out of the pool. Every time I get tired or think of giving in, I think of you. You always strive to be the very best at everything you do, and I have always looked up to you. You have shown me that excellence is achievable in every aspect of life, and that is something I take with me in all that I set out to do—because of you.

Eli, I usually refer to you as my "should've been twin," we just happened to be born two years apart. You and I have shared quite the journey from the double stroller days to the football in the hallway disaster and everything in between. I cannot express how proud I am of you. I can't help but look at you and think of that little kid who just loved swimming fast and winning blue ribbons—he would go on to become a D1 NCAA swim captain at an ACC school, Olympic Trials qualifier, and now on your way to flight school. You are also the most kind-hearted person I have ever known, and you make me want to be more like you.

I feel blessed to have two built-in best friends for life in you guys. I am proud of all that you have both accomplished—you inspire me to be the best version of myself. I could not have done or achieved any of this without you. I love you guys.

Thank you to all of my extended family and friends. Especially all of my aunts, uncles, cousins, and my God Parents, Stephanie and Mike. I feel so blessed to have such an incredible and loving family. To have so much support behind me is everything. I love you all.

To my friends in Clarkesville and Toccoa, GA—thank you. You have all touched and impacted my journey. I would not be who I am today without you. It is amazing to know that I have an army of supporters right there behind me when I step up to race. I may travel the world and move to different places, but in my heart, I will always be that small-town Georgia girl with friends who feel more like family. How lucky am I that I will always have a place and community like that to call home? You have all believed in me from the very start, and I cannot express my gratitude for that.

I want to thank all of my amazing doctors and medical team who feel more like family, especially my physical therapist, Dr. Colleen Coulter-O'Berry, who was there from the beginning. Thank you for not only being my incredible physical therapist who made me stronger and more fearless but for giving us hope. Alongside Colleen, I also want to thank my orthopedic surgeon, Dr. Jill Flanagan. Dr. Flanagan and I met for the first time back in 2011, and ever since, she has been there every step of the way and has helped me in my most challenging moments. I cannot tell you how often I've called Dr. Flanagan, sometimes from an ER, asking her what to do or getting an opinion of what she thinks is broken or needs surgery. Dr. Flanagan has selflessly moved her schedule around or made time to see me when things have gone wrong, and she is always on board, reassuring me that whatever we're facing, we will get through to the other side. I will never be able to thank either of these amazing professionals enough for all that they have done and continue to do for me and all OI patients who walk through their doors. To know them and be under their treatment is a gift that I am so fortunate to experience.

Two very special individuals introduced me to the world of paraswimming, and if it weren't for them, I might not have ever discovered and set out to chase this dream. The day swimming officials Glenda Orth and the late Pete Junkins approached me on the pool deck is forever ingrained in my mind because it changed the trajectory of my life and career. Over the years, having the opportunity to share the deck with them has been a great honor, especially at Games with Glenda right there as I won gold—that was indeed a full-circle moment. I only wish I could talk to Pete one more time and thank him for all he has done for me, but I know he is always there on the deck, in spirit.

Swimming competitively teaches countless lessons applicable to everyday life circumstances. Many life lessons come from the selfless coaches who work day in and day out on that pool deck alongside you. To my very first coach and head coach of the Habersham Rapids, Anthony Rabern—thank you for giving me my start. When I ditched the life jacket and swam those laps with you at the side, clapping and cheering me on, I can't imagine what that must've taken for you to do that. To welcome a little girl with many differences onto your team and treat her like any other is an extraordinary thing, and you will always have my unwavering gratitude. Thank you for teaching me to look beyond someone's differences and always to see their potential within.

There was one coach along the way who was always more than just that: my "moach" (that's Mom and coach combined). My mom came into the coaching picture when I desperately needed a change in those who were guiding me in the water. She worked tirelessly to construct workouts, find pool space, and learn as much as she could every day to make sure I had the tools I needed to succeed. She was the one who got me not only on my first national team but onto my first Games team in 2012 and into collegiate swimming. I can never thank her enough for all she did as my Moach. I am proud to see her owning and operating her team today, coaching other kids to achieving their dreams. Mom, thank you for teaching me the value of work ethic and never allowing what others say or their doubts to stop me from pursuing my goals.

It was August 2014 when I started my collegiate career at Loyola under head coach Brian Loeffler. To say I was intimidated by Brian in those first few weeks is an understatement which is funny to think back on now. After my first whole week of classes and Brian's workouts, I remember collapsing on my bed in absolute exhaustion, wondering how I would make it through four years of that routine. Through not only my four years of collegiate swimming but also my two years of post-grad swimming with Brian, we came to know and understand one another very well. Brian became part of my family and has seen me on my very worst days—bad practices and injuries included, but he has never stopped believing in me. Brian, in my opinion, is one of the most gifted, successful, and intelligent coaches on the pool deck, but he is also one of the most humble and kind individuals you will ever meet.

Brian, I will never be able to thank you enough for coaching me to 3 golds and a silver in Rio, for giving me the chance to swim as a Greyhound on a Division 1 program, and most of all, for seeing me as more than just an athlete. Along the way, you have taught me that, yes, what happens in the water is important and that striving for greatness is key in every workout, but it matters more who you are on the pool deck. I will never be able to express my gratitude to you and your family for making me feel so welcomed in Baltimore.

To my Baltimore strength and lift coaches, Frank Rosenthal and Deanna Ballard, thank you. When we first started working together in 2019, in one of our first lifts, I said I wanted to do pull-ups, which I had never done before, being that I was scared of the bar height and the idea of falling. You guys made that happen for me, and they are now one of my favorite exercises. Thank you for giving me the confidence and strength in the weight room that I could take and translate over into the water. You made me see lifting in a whole new light, and for that, I am forever grateful.

Thank you to all of the support out here at the Colorado Springs Olympic and Paralympic Training Center. A huge thanks to US National Team and Resident Program Head Coach Nathan Manley for the opportunity to train out here on the Road to Tokyo. Nathan is one of the most analytical coaches I have ever had the privilege to train with. Over my time here, I have learned and developed so much within my stroke and confidence. Nathan is unique in that he makes you take a step back and think through not only the set but every stroke by what you're doing and why you're doing it. There is a reason behind everything, and he has taught me that the smallest tweaks can make huge differences, and because of that, I am a better athlete. In addition, I want to thank all of my strength and conditioning coaches in the Springs: Tyler Courtney, Janessa Schulte, Jared Siegmund, and Sam Gardner. Lifting with you all has been a great experience, and I've never felt stronger and more confident in my abilities in the weight room.

Just as we learn from coaches, we swimmers also learn from our teammates and friends on the deck. Swimming has given me so much, but I think the best part is the relationships I've formed. From traveling the country and world to represent Team USA, to swimming with my Lady Hounds at Loyola, and being Team Captain at the Cumming Waves Swim Team, I have crossed paths with truly remarkable individuals. These extraordinary people have helped not only shape who I am but helped get me to this point. To my entire swim family, thank you. All of the trips, hugs, and practice moments are what I will remember most throughout my career and life. I am so grateful for you all and wouldn't be here today without your support.

A huge thank you to my agent, Cejih Yung. I remember on our very first phone call when Cejih asked me what my goals and dreams were, I *very hesitantly* mentioned at the end of my goal list that I dreamt of writing a book one day. I couldn't even believe I said that out loud, but he went with it and said we'd make it happen someday. I cannot thank you enough for giving me the opportunity of a lifetime and always seeing the potential within me and my abilities as your first Paralympic athlete with CG Sports Company. It's been a crazy ride, and I cannot wait to see all that is still to come.

One of the most humbling and rewarding parts of my professional swimming career has been the support of incredible companies and sponsors.

To Adidas and Adidas Swim, thank you for believing in me, accepting me for who I am, and valuing me both as an athlete and as McKenzie. I am honored to live the 3-Stripe life and represent a company that aligns with the things I care about most.

To Numotion, being a lifelong customer-turned-Numotion-athlete has been the greatest full-circle moment of my career. You give people the freedom of mobility every day, and I am proud to represent that mission. Everyone deserves the independence to pursue their passions.

To LendingTree, being part of Team LendingTree has been such a fun and rewarding experience. I am forever grateful for the opportunity to work with the entire LendingTree team.

To my wonderful co-author, Holly Neumann, you kept me on track and made writing my first book an incredible experience. From our first conversation, I knew we were on the same wavelength and shared the same goal-oriented work ethic to make *Breaking Free* something special. Your guidance and reassurance, when things got tough that one day, that we would have it in our hands, is what kept me going. You are so talented and helped me put into words what has been a crazy and incredible lifelong journey. Not to mention, you absolutely deserve a gold medal for putting up with me. I am blessed to work alongside you and to have a new friend for life.

Thank you to the entire CG Sports Publishing team, especially Mike Nicloy and Matt Amerlan. I appreciate your answers to any and every question that came about—literally flooding both of your inboxes regularly. Thank you for guiding me through this process and bringing my vision to life. I also want to thank my editors, Marla McKenna and Lyda Rose Haerle, and thank you to Nicole Wurtele for the cover design of *Breaking Free*. I am forever grateful to you all.

When it came time to consider the foreword and afterword in *Breaking Free*, I thought about those who have significantly impacted my career and life. It didn't take long to come up with two of the most amazing individuals that I have had the great pleasure of knowing. To Brian Loeffler and Dr. Kara Ayers, thank you for your extraordinary contributions to *Breaking Free*. To have two of the most significant influences in my life write such kind and thoughtful words is truly humbling. I am forever indebted to you both.

I am eternally grateful to all who helped make this dream a reality.

About the Author

McKenzie Coan

McKenzie Coan is a professional swimmer, public speaker, disability advocate, and author.

She first took to the water for aqua therapy to help with her osteogenesis imperfecta (brittle bone disease). But it wasn't long after her brothers joined a swim team that she declared her days in the "baby pool" over. McKenzie joined the team, too, and she began Paralympic swimming just a few years later, at the age of 8. She loved growing up on the pool deck and, as a young swimmer, she could often be found racing around the blocks in her pink wheelchair or painting her nails while listening to Hannah Montana with her friends before a big race.

She made her first U.S. Paralympic national team at 15 in 2012 and has been a part of Team USA every year since. She competed in the 2012 Paralympic Games in London, and in 2016, she won four medals in Rio de Janeiro, including three gold. She is a six-time World Champion and two-time world record holder in the category S7 800-meter and 1500-meter freestyles. McKenzie is also an Adidas-sponsored athlete, one of the first with a physical disability to be fully sponsored by the brand.

Outside of the water, McKenzie thrives on connecting with others and sharing her story through public-speaking engagements and through Kenzie Kares, an organization she founded as a teenager to help bring hope and happiness to children who are hospitalized. She first discovered her love of public speaking as a Girl Scout, finding the same adrenaline rush on stage that she craves in the pool. She credits her time as Girl Scout, too, with fostering her competitive nature—no one could outsell her during cookie season!

McKenzie is an avid Clemson University athletics fan and can be found cheering on the Tiger basketball team every chance she gets. She holds a bachelor's degree in political science from Loyola University Maryland, where she was on the school's NCAA Div. I swim team and was a student member of the campus ADA Compliance Committee.

She will enter law school at Rutgers in 2022, where she intends to focus on civil rights and disability advocacy, inspired by her work with Kenzie Kares to act on behalf of others with disabilities, and inspired, as well, by the character Elle Woods from her favorite movie, *Legally Blonde*.

McKenzie plans to train and compete while in law school, with the goal of representing Team USA at the Paris 2024 and Los Angeles 2028 Paralympic Games. She currently lives at the Olympic and Paralympic Training Center in Colorado Springs, in anticipation of the Tokyo 2020 Games, which were postponed to August 2021 due to the coronavirus pandemic.

About the Co-Author

Holly Neumann

Holly Neumann is a writer, editor, swim instructor, and swim coach.

She got her professional start as a sportswriter covering her college swim team, and she went on to have a career as a newspaper editor and copy editor at a major West Coast daily. When her children were young, she switched gears to aquatics and water safety, and for five years, she led a nationwide adult learn-to-swim education initiative.

She loves teaching children to flip turn and dive and helping adults to feel confident and happy in the water. She lives in Florida with her family, where she enjoys open water swimming, roller skating, and chips and salsa. She occasionally posts to her blog, This Is How We Miss the Bus, but she usually forgets. This is her first book.

CPSIA information can be obtained
at www.ICGtesting.com
Printed in the USA
BVHW040457171221
623983BV00006B/135